"Think you know how you come across? Think again. Using a brilliant combination of stories and science, Heidi Grant Halvorson reveals the gulf between how others perceive us and how we perceive ourselves. But instead of leaving us to lament, she shows us how to contend with this sometimes harsh reality. This is a smart, fascinating, and eminently practical book."

—Daniel H. Pink, author, *To Sell Is Human* and *Drive: The Surprising Truth About What Motivates Us*

"This is a great book. It's important, it's riveting, and it's extremely useful. In fact, it's essential for anyone who wants to thrive in their social or business world."

—Carol S. Dweck, Lewis and Virginia Eaton Professor of Psychology, Stanford University

"Heidi's tone and smarts made this book impossible to put down."

—David Rock, Director and CEO, NeuroLeadership Institute

"Despite your best intentions, your perceptions of people are a mirage, contaminated by your past experiences, needs, and desires. This book will help you see yourself and others accurately—perhaps for the first time."

—Scott Barry Kaufman, Scientific Director, Imagination Institute, Positive Psychology Center, University of Pennsylvania

"Heidi Grant Halvorson explores the fascinating research on personal perception. Not only will this book help you to present yourself more effectively, it will also allow you to see the people around you more accurately."

—Art Markman, Annabel Iron Worsham Centennial Professor of Psychology, University of Texas at Austin; author, *Smart Thinking* and *Smart Change*

"There are so many good reasons to read this book. It's smart. It's insightful. It's helpful. But the best reason might just be that it's fun. Heidi Grant Halvorson is a great writer—wise, knowledgeable, and charming at the same time. I found myself laughing while I was learning."

—Peter Bregman, CEO, Bregman Partners; author, *18 Minutes: Find Your Focus, Master Distraction, and Get the Right Things Done*

"There is deep power in knowing how to have people see you as *only* you are."

—Nilofer Merchant, author, *11 Rules for Creating Value in the Social Era*

"Being an authentic leader means being perceived authentically. Halvorson masterfully combines research and story to outline why we're misunderstood and how to be seen for who we really are."

—David Burkus, author, *The Myths of Creativity*

"This is a code book for deciphering one of the great riddles of life: why don't others see us as we see ourselves? With fascinating facts and memorable examples, renowned psychologist Heidi Grant Halvorson shows us the path to making a better impression on others while maintaining a sense of integrity."

—Adam Grant, Class of 1965 Chaired Professor of Management, Wharton School, University of Pennsylvania; *New York Times* bestselling author, *Give and Take*

"The best book ever written on why it is so difficult for us humans to communicate with others and what we can do about it. I was blown away by the masterful weave of stories, rock-solid evidence, and, especially, advice that I can use *right now* to get my message across without confusing or pissing off the other people in my life."

— Robert I. Sutton, Professor of Management Science and Engineering, Stanford University; author, *The No Asshole Rule*

NO ONE
UNDERSTANDS
YOU

**AND
WHAT TO DO
ABOUT IT**

NO ONE UNDERSTANDS YOU

AND WHAT TO DO ABOUT IT

Heidi Grant Halvorson

Harvard Business Review Press

Boston, Massachusetts

Copyright 2015 Heidi Grant Halvorson
All rights reserved
Printed in the United States of America

10 9 8 7 6 5 4 3 2 1

No part of this publication may be reproduced, stored in or introduced into a retrieval system, or transmitted, in any form, or by any means (electronic, mechanical, photocopying, recording, or otherwise), without the prior permission of the publisher. Requests for permission should be directed to permissions@hbsp.harvard.edu, or mailed to Permissions, Harvard Business School Publishing, 60 Harvard Way, Boston, Massachusetts 02163.

The web addresses referenced in this book were live and correct at the time of the book's publication but may be subject to change.

Library of Congress Cataloging-in-Publication Data

Halvorson, Heidi Grant-, 1973-
    No one understands you and what to do about it / Heidi Grant Halvorson.
    pages cm
    ISBN 978-1-62527-412-0 (paperback)
    1. Interpersonal communication.   2. Self-presentation.   3. Interpersonal relations.   4. Social perception.   I. Title.
    BF637.C45H2817 2015
    158.2—dc23

2014037107

The paper used in this publication meets the requirements of the American National Standard for Permanence of Paper for Publications and Documents in Libraries and Archives Z39.48-1992.

Contents

Introduction

How They See You, How They Don't

Whatever you may have heard to the contrary, Chip Wilson is not an idiot. The founder and former CEO and chairman of Lululemon Athletica is, in point of fact, a highly successful entrepreneur, philanthropist, innovator, and self-made billionaire. Idiots are very rarely any of those things.

But a 2013 Bloomberg TV interview with him and his wife Shannon, Lululemon's original athletic wear designer, was not one of his finest moments. When he was asked about reports of customers complaining about "pilling" in the company's newest line of high-end yoga pants, he defensively replied that "some women's bodies just actually don't work" for yoga pants and that the problem was "really about the rubbing through the thighs, how much pressure is there." Translation: *If your fat thighs are ruining your pricey Lululemon yoga pants, that's your problem. Maybe my pants are not for you.* (Incidentally, if you watch the video, you will see Shannon Wilson shoot him a look at that moment that would have surely turned him to stone had he noticed it, which he did not.)

As Elizabeth Harris, reporting for the *New York Times*, later put it with gleeful understatement, "Perhaps going on television and suggesting that women with large thighs were not the ideal customer—at least when it comes to yoga pants—would never be considered advisable for the top executive of an athletic wear company."

Wilson's comment was, of course, horribly offensive—but was it Chip Wilson's intention to be offensive? Did he even think what he said was offensive? In a video apology he later issued before stepping down as Lululemon's chairman—a statement that seemed to be more aimed at Lululemon employees than the customers whose thighs he had impugned—Wilson said that he was "sad for the repercussions of my actions" and that he "accepted responsibility," that ubiquitous postdisaster PR phrase that everyone repeats but no one ever seems to mean. But nowhere did he actually acknowledge that there was anything wrong with what he had said or that he personally had been wrong to say it.

I'm going to go out on a limb and suggest that Chip Wilson did not intend, with those poorly chosen words, to insult and alienate his loyal customer base. (Or to seriously irritate his wife.) It just doesn't make sense to assume otherwise. So, if that wasn't his intention, and if he's not an idiot (self-made billionaire, people), then what happened?

. . .

About a year ago, I was brainstorming ideas for my next book, and I'll be honest—none of them were winners. I never cease to be intrigued by the steady stream of new findings and theories that are emerging in my field, so it's not that I couldn't find anything interesting to write about. It's that interesting just isn't enough. Readers of the kinds of books that I write expect to be enlightened *and* equipped with practical, effective strategies they can use in their professional and personal lives. They want knowledge in action, and rightly so. And none of the ideas I was coming up with seemed particularly useful or compelling.

So I did something I've never done before . . . I asked my husband. You see, my husband is a very successful and brilliant executive who never, ever reads books on management, innovation, motivation, influence, or any of the kinds of things people like me write about. He hasn't even read *my* books. Which is why I thought that if I could find a topic that even he would be interested in reading, I might really have something.

"If you were ever going to pick up a book like the ones I write, what would it be about? What would you want to know?" I asked him.

He thought about this for a few moments and replied, "I suppose the one problem I haven't figured out a good solution for—the one that keeps coming up again and again—is how I come across to other people. I get the feeling that sometimes people think I'm being critical, or aloof, or disengaged, and that's not at all my intention. But I don't know how to fix it, because I don't understand what they are seeing. If there was a book about that, one that was based on evidence and not just bullshit, I would read it."

I jumped up off the couch, kissed him, and ran to my office to start typing—because what became clear to me as I listened to him was that this is everyone's problem, not just my husband's, or Chip Wilson's. Without the ability to consistently and accurately telegraph our thoughts and intentions to others, none of us can succeed—no individual, no team, and no organization. Communication is vital, but the great irony is that human beings have a surprisingly difficult time when it comes to knowing what exactly they are communicating.

After you have read this book, you will understand better than ever why that's the case—why communication is so very, very hard to get right. But you will also have a better understanding, perhaps for the first time, of what other people are actually seeing in your words and actions. And with that, you have the power to shape that perception—to take control of the messages you send.

When people ask me if this book is about "making a good impression," I tell them no, it isn't. Because for me, it's always been about something more essential and more authentic than that: it's about *coming across the way you intend to.* In a world where relationships are everything and no one accomplishes anything alone, could there be anything more important than that?

. . .

The uncomfortable truth is that most of us don't come across the way we intend. We can't see ourselves truly objectively, and neither can anyone else. Human beings have a strong tendency to distort other people's feedback to fit their own views. We know this intellectually, and yet we rarely seem to recognize it as it's happening.

That can cause you big problems in your personal and professional life. People may not trust you, may not like you, or may not even notice you, as a result of these errors in perception. If you have ever felt yourself underestimated or misjudged, if you have stepped on toes without meaning to and been called to task for it, if you have wanted to cry out "That's not fair!" when false and hurtful assumptions have been made about you, I'm here to tell you that you are right. The way we see one another is far from fair. In fact, much of this process of perceiving other people, as you'll soon discover, isn't even rational. It is biased, incomplete, and inflexible. It is also largely (but not entirely) automatic.

Our intuitions about how we are seen by others might be surprisingly inaccurate, but there is good news: social psychologists have been studying how we really see each other, for the better part of a century. Our collective research shows that perceivers are, without a doubt, prone to error. These kinds of errors are, however, *predictable*—perception is governed by rules and biases that we can identify and anticipate.

The aim of this book is to help you understand how other people really see you and to give you tools to alter your words and actions (when necessary) so that you can send the signals you *want* to send. It will describe the persistent errors we all make and how to fix them. Knowing how you are actually perceived—in an interview, on a sales call, in your everyday interactions with your boss or coworkers—can go a long way toward improving nearly every aspect of your working life. It's the key to making—and sustaining—a good impression, to being respected and valued, to getting ahead, and, as Chip Wilson now no doubt knows, to hanging on to what you've got.

My hope is that after you read this book, many of your past misunderstandings will begin to make sense. Best of all, you'll be able to communicate more effectively, renew and strengthen your relationships, be recognized for the person you truly are, and, when it matters most, come across the way you intend to.

In part I, I'll lay out the basics of how perception works, including the two main phases to perception, Phase 1 (automatic and filled with bias) and Phase 2 (effortful and more accurate). In part II, we'll unpack the major lenses of perception that shape these biases—trust, power, and ego. In part III, we'll see how the personality of perceivers can influence what they see and how they see it. Part IV discusses what to do if you've come across in a way you didn't intend. There are a few things you can do to encourage your perceiver to see you more accurately and some steps you can take to become a more accurate judge of others. However, if it seems as if I'm spending a lot of time on the aspects of perception that fall outside of your direct control, you're right: one terrifying message of this book is how warped other people's perceptions of you may be, despite your best intentions. But the good news is that understanding how perception really works will give you a lot more ability to shape others' perceptions—without their even realizing it.

So how does perception really work? Let's find out.

Part I

Why It's So Hard to Understand Each Other

Chapter 1

You Are Surprisingly Hard to Understand

The president thought it had all gone rather well.[1] In fact, he left the stage after his first debate with Mitt Romney thinking himself the victor. He'd followed his and his team's plan to appear steady, resolute, "presidential." His aides feared that getting into an angry exchange would damage his likability, and the president himself decided to avoid the one-liners his team had prepared for him, not wanting to look snarky. His plan was to stay above the fray and refuse to take the bait.[2]

He was shocked to later learn the truth: the audience thought that he was lethargic and disengaged. He had allowed his opponent to go on the offensive and stay there, barely fighting back as Romney landed one hit after another. Barack Obama's debate performance had been a disaster, and even his staunchest allies thought so. A CNN/Opinion Research Poll taken right after the debate showed that 67 percent of viewers thought Romney had won, whereas only 25 percent had thought Obama had.

How could someone with Barack Obama's obvious gifts as a public speaker so utterly fail to grasp how he was coming across to his audience? Why did he need his aides to tell him afterward what was so clear to everyone else in the auditorium?

It is unlikely that President Obama was feeling lethargic and disengaged in the middle of a nationally televised debate, with his presidency very much on the line. And while most of us won't engage in presidential debates over the course of our careers, most of us do fall prey to the same sort of trap.

Statistically speaking, there are only weak correlations between how others see us and how we believe we are seen. And while I don't actually know what your colleagues, your partner, or anyone else thinks of you—I do know that you don't know, either. Oh sure, you might be getting some of it right, but I promise you that you are getting a lot of it wrong. Without realizing it, you—like everyone else—are very likely operating under two very flawed assumptions: first, that other people see you objectively as you are, and, second, that other people see you as you see yourself.

Both assumptions are flawed for two simple reasons.

Reason Number One: You Are a Riddle, Wrapped in an Enigma

For starters, you are much harder to read than you might imagine. No one is actually an open book. For you to be truly, completely, and 100 percent accurately knowable, other people would need to be able to look into your mind directly. Recent advances in neuroscience notwithstanding, that's not possible. So you will, of necessity, remain something of a mystery to everyone around you.

And you aren't doing as much as you might imagine to make yourself knowable, either. Your emotions are less obvious than you realize, and your face is less expressive, too. Studies show that while very strong, basic emotions—surprise, fear, disgust, and anger—are fairly easy to read, the more subtle emotions we experience on a daily basis are not. Chances are, how you look when you are slightly frustrated isn't all that different from how you look when you are a little concerned, confused, disappointed, or nervous. Your "I'm kind of hurt by what you just said" face probably looks an awful lot like your "I'm not at all hurt by what you just said" face. And the majority of times that you've said to yourself, "I made my intentions clear," or "He knows what I meant," you didn't and he doesn't.

Psychologists call this the *transparency illusion*, and we are all its victims. Take, for instance, research by Jacquie Vorauer and Stephanie-Danielle Claude of the University of Manitoba. They were interested in how readily negotiators would pick up on the goals and intentions of their negotiation partners— obviously, a critical piece of information in any negotiation. The researchers observed pairs of negotiators who were asked to jointly solve an interpersonal problem that had no obvious or easy solution, such as: "Your sister is engaged to marry a man who, in your opinion, is bad news. You do not trust him, and you suspect that he has been cheating on your sister. Your sister, however, is very much in love. What should you do?"[3]

Before beginning to work out joint solutions to each of the problems, negotiators were asked to privately indicate which of the following five goals was their primary goal in the negotiation:

1. Hold firm to my own personal opinions.

2. Make sure that the other person feels satisfied with the chosen solutions, even if it means that I have to compromise some of my own values and beliefs.

3. Make sure that each of us makes a similar number of compromises.

4. Focus on identifying the best solutions to the problems without worrying about the implications of my choices for my relationships with the other person.

5. Gain the liking of the other person.

At the end of the negotiations, the participants were asked what they thought their partner's primary goal was, based on the way he or she behaved throughout the task. How transparent was the partner's true intention? Evidently, about as transparent as a brick wall, as it was guessed correctly only 26 percent of the time—just barely better than chance. Now, how transparent did each partner believe his or her intentions to be? The partners estimated that their goal would be crystal clear 60 percent of the time.

And yet no one is entirely unknowable either. In fact, some of us are actually easier to understand than others. These people seem to express themselves in ways that allow others to perceive them more accurately. Psychologists refer to this ability as being more or less *judgeable*, or as personality expert David Funder calls it, being a "good target." What actually makes someone more judgeable? Funder has argued that in order for people to be accurate in their assessments of someone else, four things need to happen. The target must (1) make information *available* and (2) make sure that information is *relevant*. Then, the perceiver must (3) *detect*, or pay attention to, that information and (4) *use* it correctly.[4]

Let's focus for now on the parts that are in your (i.e., the target's) control. (The other parts, about how perceivers detect and use information, will be the focus of the next chapter.) To be judgeable, you are going to need to make information about yourself available to others, and it should provide evidence of the particular qualities you are trying to convey. (In other words, just knowing that you graduated at the top of your class at Harvard tells me nothing at all about how personable, trustworthy, creative, or resilient you are.) So if you are a very shy and reserved person who reveals next to nothing about your thoughts and feelings to the people around you, then they will know very little about you—aside from the fact that you are shy and reserved, obviously. The danger there is that people will generally fill in the blanks themselves, imagining a whole personality profile for you that may or may not—probably not—be accurate.

Manipulative people can use this dynamic to their advantage. For instance, I had an office mate in graduate school who was famous for his reserve in romantic relationships. Actually, he was fairly reserved in general, but when it came to dating, he managed to somehow say or do almost nothing that would reveal his true thoughts and feelings. He was a completely closed book. I once asked him if this caused problems for him with the women in his life, and he told me, with remarkable candor, that he did it intentionally—he had found that women would usually interpret his silences in positive ways. (*He's so mysterious. He's a deep thinker. Maybe he's been hurt before— I'll bet he's really sensitive . . .*) The personality they would invent for him, he said, was in fact much better than his actual personality. So to him, silence was golden. As a psychologist,

I found this fascinating. As a single woman, on the other hand, I found it more than a little terrifying.

Ignoring my former office mate for the moment, it is definitely better to be judgeable—to have other people read you easily and accurately. Research consistently shows that people who are more judgeable are psychologically better adjusted—they are happier; are more satisfied with their personal and professional lives; have more lasting, positive relationships; and have a greater sense of purpose.[5] They feel able to live more authentically and are more confident in their self-knowledge. This makes a lot of sense. If people are seeing you the way you see yourself, then you aren't getting all the unsettling, self-doubt-inducing feedback that the chronically misunderstood have to endure. Life is simply easier and more rewarding when people "get you" and provide you with the opportunities and support that are a good fit for you.

Reason Number Two: Your Actions Are a Matter of Interpretation

The second reason those core assumptions—that you are seen objectively and are seen the way you see yourself—are flawed is that the information other people get from you and about you, the words you speak and the behaviors you engage in, is always given meaning through interpretation.

That can be hard to wrap your head around, because it's not at all how perception feels. It feels like we see what is there—like there's no interpretation involved.

Imagine that your neighbor Steve runs into you at the grocery store and says, "Hi! So glad to see you!" That seems unambiguous, doesn't it? It obviously means he is feeling happy to see you because he genuinely likes you—unless, of course, he means it sarcastically. (*Was there a funny tone in his voice? Was he looking away when he said it?*) Or maybe he's just pretending to be happy because he wants something from you. (*Is it the end of the month? Steve is usually broke at the end of the month . . .*) Then again, maybe he's just being polite. (*Hmmm . . .*)

OK, now imagine that you and Steve have started chatting in the produce aisle. But he keeps staring off into the distance. That is clearly rude, isn't it? Steve is obviously a jerk. Unless maybe something is on his mind. (*Didn't someone say his mother has been ill?*) Or maybe he's distracted. (*After all, he is in the middle of running errands.*)

Strings of words, like *Hi-I'm-so-glad-to-see-you*, and actions, like staring off into the distance, are the clues we have to try to understand what another person is like. But as you can see, these word strings and actions have very little meaning by themselves. We need to figure out what they mean—from the context and from everything else we know (or think we know) about the person. So if you believe that Steve likes you, then Steve's greeting will seem friendly and genuine. If, on the other hand, you feel like Steve's been giving you the cold shoulder for a while now, you are likely to doubt his sincerity or wonder if he's about to ask you to feed his cat while he's away.

So if words and deeds must be interpreted to give them meaning, you can never be seen as you "objectively" are (and neither can Steve). And since you have unique access to your own thoughts and intentions, while other people are left having to guess what you are up to, it's easy to see why those interpretations can end up being very different—why other people don't see you the way you see yourself.

In fact, other people don't even agree with each other about what you are like. I'll bet President Obama thinks of himself as a highly competent person—after all, the man has two Ivy League degrees, served as editor of the *Harvard Law Review*, and was skillful enough to be elected senator and then president. But do others see him that way? A 2012 Pew poll asked one thousand Americans to describe the president in one word. There was enormous variety in the words people chose—with the popularity of words like "great" and "intelligent" being roughly equal to words like "failure" and "incompetent." Equal numbers of people described him as "honest" and "a liar." (And then there's poor Vice President Joe Biden—the most popular word used to describe him was "good," followed very closely by "idiot.")

It's really not that there is *no* agreement on the character traits of public figures. It's just that there's a lot less than you think. For example, a group of research psychologists asked over two hundred Germans to judge the personalities of fifteen well-known public figures in Germany. These included Pope Benedict XVI, actress Angelina Jolie, former Italian prime minister Silvio Berlusconi, designer Karl Lagerfeld, and singer Madonna.[6] The participants in the study were given a list of thirty adjectives (e.g., reckless, helpful, lively, selfish, responsible, shy, irritable) to use to describe each celebrity.

The researchers found that among people who actually liked the celebrity in question, the average judgment correlation was 0.67. In other words, there was substantial agreement about what someone was like among those who viewed that person positively. (Quick correlation refresher: A correlation of 1.0 is perfect, meaning that one thing exactly predicts the other—they are in total sync. The closer you are to 1.0, the stronger the relationship. A correlation of 0, on the other hand, means there is no relationship at all between the two things you are comparing.)

Among those who were more neutral about the celebrity, the correlation fell to 0.44, and among those who actively disliked the celebrity, it was only 0.33, indicating significant differences of opinion. To borrow a bit from Tolstoy, it would appear that while all your fans see you similarly, the haters each hate you in their own, unique way.

You could argue that differences of perception should be expected with public figures, because we don't actually know them personally. We know them through their TV and film appearances, their magazine interviews, their Twitter and Facebook feeds. We know them through the opinions of talking heads, cultural critics, and gossip mongers.

But surely someone who knows you firsthand will see the real you—the self that you see, right? To answer that question, researchers asked nearly four hundred college roommates to describe their own personality along with their roommate's, to see if actually knowing each other, along with time spent living together, would have an impact on perception.[7] Specifically, they wanted to see if over time, your roommate was more likely to begin to see you the way you see yourself. The answer was yes: as long as you have lived together for a minimum of *nine* months. It takes that long for perceptions to even begin to get in sync.

And even then, the correlations between how college students saw themselves and how their roommates saw them were surprisingly low, in the 0.2 to 0.5 range. Perceptions among female roommates were more similar than among male roommates, though it wasn't exactly clear why. It may be that women are more accurate perceivers, or it may be that women have a better sense of how they are perceived—in other words, that their sense of who they are is more influenced by how others see them. In general, research shows women to be (on average) more socially sensitive and more concerned with interpersonal relationships than men, so it makes sense that women would be more invested in seeing others accurately and in how they themselves are seen. Nevertheless, even among women, the correlations between how they see themselves and how others see them were modest at best.

What about people who really know each other—like married couples? They share a life together, experience the same ups and downs, the same joys and worries, and (usually) sleep in the same bed. Surely, with all that intimate knowledge of you, your husband or wife must see you the way you see yourself, right?

Alas. There are, in fact, significant differences in perception among spouses, too. Interestingly, these differences are also highly predictable. These biases were nicely illustrated in a study of forty-four married couples, roughly half of whom were currently in marriage counseling. Those in counseling (or, as the researchers referred to them, the "distressed" group) were more likely to have a negative bias—they saw their partner in a far less flattering light than the partner did and tended to hold the partner more personally responsible for any bad behaviors they had engaged in.[8] So while Larry may see himself as a fairly conscientious guy who occasionally forgets to take the garbage out (who doesn't?), his wife, Susan, sees him as irresponsible and inconsiderate, leaving her (once again) to pick up the slack.

The couples who were not in counseling—the "nondistressed" group—tended to have a positive bias and were more forgiving. So when Bob forgets to take out the garbage, Mary sees him as merely a bit absent-minded, but really that's understandable given how hard Bob has been working, and really, brilliant people are often a little absent-minded, aren't they?

Now, maybe Susan is right and Mary is being a fool. I'm not saying that one of these biases is right and the other is wrong—in fact, any bias is by definition sometimes wrong. (On the other hand, a negative bias in a marriage is apparently quite likely to land you in marriage counseling . . . so that's food for thought.) But taken together, it's easy to see why misunderstandings between friends and lovers are so common and why our relationships—the keys to our ultimate success and happiness—can be so stressful.

Now you may be asking yourself, if even married couples can't understand each other—and if even the president of the United States, with his team of communications professionals, doesn't come across the way he intends to—what hope do I have of ever getting my boss to see my potential, or my colleague to see how hard I work? The next step is to understand how little we actually pay attention to each other and how much we rely on assumptions. That's the subject of the next chapter.

Key Takeaways

- We don't communicate nearly as much information as we think we do. When you say, "He knows what I meant" or "I made myself clear," chances are, he doesn't and you didn't. Our faces are not nearly as expressive as we think they are; mild boredom can look an awful lot like mild interest or mild concern.

- We fall prey to two assumptions: (1) that other people see us *objectively as we are* and (2) that other people see us *as we see ourselves*. In fact, our perceivers don't even agree with each other on what they see in us.

- There are two main reasons we're so hard to understand: First, no one is actually an open book. And second, our actions are always subject to interpretation.

Chapter 2

Your Observers Are Cognitive Misers (and So Are You)

In the 1980s, psychologists Susan Fiske and Shelly Taylor were looking for a way to describe what research was showing to be a ubiquitous tendency among humans: to think only as much as they feel they need to, and no more. And so the metaphor of the *cognitive miser* was born, with each of us an Ebenezer Scrooge—except instead of sitting on piles of money and refusing to pay for an extra lump of coal to keep the house warm, we sit on reserves of mental energy and processing capacity, unwilling to spend much of it unless we really have to. We rely on simple, efficient thought processes to get the job done—not so much out of laziness (though there is some of that, too), but out of necessity. There is just too much going on, too much to notice, understand, and act on, for us to give every individual and every occurrence our undivided, unbiased attention. So not only are you innately hard to understand, but the people observing you are hoarding their attention.

Human thought, like every other complex process, is subject to the speed-versus-accuracy trade-off. Go fast, and you make mistakes. Be thorough and diligent, and you take an eternity. We are, as Fiske later called us, *motivated tacticians*—strategically choosing ease and speed, or effort and accuracy, depending on our motivation. Most of the time, just the gist will do, so we choose speed.

The cognitive miser's favorite shortcut tools are *heuristics* and *assumptions*. Heuristics are rules of thumb like "Things that come to mind easily happen more frequently." In other words, if I ask you, "Does your Uncle Phil lose his temper a lot?" and you can remember a lot of times when your Uncle Phil lost his temper, then you will probably conclude that yes, Phil loses his temper quite often. But if you have a hard time recalling such an instance, you would conclude that Phil is gentle like a lamb. Like most rules of thumb, this heuristic will steer you toward the right answer much of the time. But it can also lead you astray.

Quick—which is more common, getting struck by lightning or getting bitten by a shark? Most people think shark bites are more frequent, when in fact roughly five thousand people in the United States are struck by lightning each year, compared with only ten to fifteen who are attacked by sharks. (On the National Geographic Shark Week website, I also learned the fun fact that in 1996, only thirteen people were injured by sharks, while forty-three thousand were injured by toilets, and twenty-six hundred by room fresheners.)[1]

Why do we think sharks are a much bigger source of danger than lightning strikes and toilets and room fresheners? Because whenever someone is bitten by a shark, you hear about it on the news. There's something so primally terrifying about shark attacks (thank you, Steven Spielberg) that it makes for a great infotainment story. When is the last time you saw a story about a lightning victim on the news, or a guy who fell and hit his head on the toilet lid, or . . . I'm honestly not sure how you get injured by a room freshener, but you see my point.

Assumptions, the cognitive miser's other favorite shortcut, come in many varieties, too. They guide what the perceiver sees, how that information is interpreted, and how it is remembered—forming an integral part of his or her perception of you. In the rest of this chapter, I'll describe how some of the most powerful and pervasive of these assumptions work.

Confirmation Bias and the Primacy Effect

Perhaps the most prevalent, and most influential, of all the assumptions that guide perception is this: when other people look at you, they see what they expect to see. Psychologists call this *confirmation bias*.

If people have reason to believe that you are smart, they will see evidence of intelligence in your behavior—whether or not there is any. If they have reason to believe you are dishonest, they will interpret a lack of eye contact or awkward body language as evidence that you have something to hide—as opposed to evidence that you are shy, or distracted, or in gastric distress.

Confirmation bias is shaped by many factors. Stereotypes about the groups to which you belong, your apparent similarity to other people the perceivers know, and culture (yours *and* theirs) are among the most consequential. And of course, their own past experience with you, if they have any, plays a major role.

That last part seems fairly logical, as far as assumptions go. If you have been gregarious, pessimistic, or hot-headed in the past, it's reasonable to think you are likely to continue to be so in the future and to interpret your behavior accordingly. If you say something that could be considered offensive or humorous, and I know you to be a jokester, then I'm more likely to go with the latter interpretation and to see the humor in your off-color remark. My past experience with you helps me to make the right call.

The problem, however, is that our early impressions of a person can hold far too much weight and can lead us astray when they paint an inaccurate picture. Psychologists refer to this as the *primacy effect*—that the information we get about a person early in our observation of him or her influences how we interpret and remember later information.

Imagine two children—each taking a thirty-question math test. On the first half, Timmy gets fourteen out of fifteen correct, while Charlotte gets only six. In the second half, the scores reverse—with Charlotte getting fourteen, and Timmy only six. Objectively, these two children have both performed at the same level—getting a total of twenty out of thirty problems correct. So rationally, anyone watching would conclude that they have the same level of mastery in math, right?

Only that's not what happens—not even close. In study after study, researchers find that Timmy is perceived—even by experts like math teachers—to be the more talented of the two.[2] This is because performance on the first half of the test exerts a far greater influence on judgment than performance on the second. In essence, when the test is only half-way finished, the perceiver has already concluded that Timmy is smart and Charlotte is not. What happens afterward does precious little to alter those initial impressions.

The implications of findings like these for late bloomers, or anyone who struggles initially only to excel later, are terrifying. It's not impossible to change these initial impressions (more on that later), but it is really difficult. Charlotte would have to present overwhelming evidence of her math ability in order to override it, while Timmy can happily coast on his early success for quite a while. The problem for Charlotte is that she may not even be given the chance to override that impression if she is placed in a remedial math track or discouraged from pursuing math altogether. Think of all the promising young actors whose first roles in terrible movies cost them a future in acting, and all those whose early successes protected them from paying the price for appearing in real stinkers. (*She Devil*, Meryl Streep? Really?)

The primacy effect is the reason your parents still treat you like you are twelve even when you are forty. In their eyes, you are still the person they first knew you to be—naive, inexperienced, and more than a little foolish. My mother still insists that I am disorganized and scatterbrained, despite the fact that I literally make my living writing and speaking about planning and time management. She constantly tells me that I should "learn to write things down." Sigh.

The primacy effect is also almost entirely responsible for the fact that sometimes, we can do no wrong in someone else's eyes, while at other times, we seem to be screwed no matter what we do—or as I like to call it, *The Ballad of Ben Stiller in Every Ben Stiller Movie*.

Poor Ben Stiller. The characters he portrays on film are generally well-intentioned, decent guys who make a bad impression in the first five minutes of the film and spend the last eighty-five minutes trying to undo the damage, with little to no success. *Meet the Parents, Night at the Museum, There's Something About Mary, Tropic Thunder*: in each, Stiller plays a man who has made some mistakes—mistakes he is really embarrassed about. Others see him as a liar, a loser, an idiot, a talentless hack. He tries again and again to make everyone see that *that's not who he really is*, but seemingly no matter what he does, it's viewed through the lens of his past behavior.

While most of us are not making bad first impressions on such a spectacular scale (thankfully), we are all subject to this kind of bias. People who know you—particularly those who know you well—will tend to see you the way they have always seen you. One of my favorite research examples of the primacy effect comes from a study that recruited pairs of close friends. Each friend was asked to describe the other's personality (privately) on a long list of dimensions—like funny, smart, creative, assertive, and so forth. Randomly, one friend was then selected to be the target, and the other the evaluator. Each target was asked to perform four tasks that the evaluator later watched via video.

The first task was ordinary enough—a game of general knowledge trivia, with difficult questions like "How high is Mount Everest?" and "How many people live in Tokyo?" The rest reads like an episode of *Whose Line Is It Anyway?* A role-play task required the target to call a "neighbor" (actually a member of the research team) and demand that they turn down the volume of their stereo. Next, the target was asked to spontaneously tell a brief story, involving the words *corkscrew, holiday, catastrophe*, and *glove box*. (Go ahead. Try it.) Last, the target sang a song of his or her choosing, told a favorite joke, and, in a final act of humiliation, had to pantomime the word *party*. I'm not sure what the participants in this study were paid, but whatever it was, it wasn't enough.

The evaluator (or the lucky one) was then asked to rate his or her friend's performance on these four tasks on a list of dimensions: How intelligent was the behavior? How funny? How creative? Compared with unbiased observers (i.e., strangers), ratings of the friend's behavior were dramatically skewed, almost uniformly reflecting their prior opinion of the friend, rather than the actual behavior displayed. In other words, even if Harry's joke was just awful or if he scored miserably on the test of trivia, Bob still thought the joke was funny if he thought of Harry as a funny guy, and Bob blamed the test (rather than Bob) for the poor performance if he thought of Bob as smart.

This, in a nutshell, is why it is so hard to get people to revise their opinions of their friends and lovers, their coworkers, or their employees. The perceivers aren't necessarily being stubborn or willfully putting blinders on—they just don't see what you see, because the assumptions guiding their perception are very different from the ones guiding yours. Something clearly inconsistent with someone's existing view of you might get some notice, but anything only moderately inconsistent with a person's existing view of you gets ignored or reinterpreted to provide a better fit. This is one of the reasons that first impressions are so important to get right and are so resistant to change after they have been formed—and that when you are looking to change someone's opinion of you, you are going to have to go big or go home.

Stereotypes

Under most circumstances, people use stereotypes about the groups to which you belong (or appear to belong) to interpret everything you do and say. And most of the time, people don't actually know they are doing it. In fact, they don't even have to believe a stereotype to be affected by it.

At its most basic, stereotyping is a form of *categorization*— something human brains have evolved to do swiftly and automatically. Categorization allows us to navigate and interact with new objects in the world with relative ease. You walk into a room you have never been in before, and you know immediately that the thing next to the table—the one with four legs and a horizontal square on top, that isn't moving and appears to be made of wood—is a chair. Imagine what a colossal pain it would be if every time you encountered a new chair, or apple, dog, or tree, you had to figure out everything about it from scratch. Like a visitor to an alien planet, every object would seem new, strange, and possibly dangerous. But instead, once you've figured out the basics of how chairs look and what they do, every new chair you encounter is a no-brainer. Even if you've never seen that particular chair before in your life, you know it's for sitting, rather than for eating or petting or climbing. You are, in fact, a world-class identifier of chairs, cars, rocks, fish, and all sorts of other things—you can do this at a glance because your brain was designed to do it.

And you have beliefs about these different categories of things, too. You believe, for instance, that rocks are hard, cars run on gasoline, and fish swim. These beliefs aren't right 100 percent of the time—a dead fish doesn't swim, and my high school boyfriend's car seemed to rarely run at all—but they are useful guidelines for knowing what kind of behavior to expect from a particular thing and how to interact with it.

Stereotypes are the beliefs we have about categories of people, and we categorize people in lots of ways: by gender, race, sexual orientation, ethnicity, profession, and socioeconomic class. Some of the beliefs associated with these categories are positive, such as *Asians are good at math* or *firefighters are brave*. Others are decidedly less so (e.g., *redheads are hot-tempered*; *women are weak*; *poor people are lazy*).

We have beliefs about categories as a result of other kinds of differences, too. Our hobbies, interests, and abilities (or lack thereof) can form the basis of stereotypes. Science-fiction fans are brainy, socially challenged, and allergic to the outdoors. Hipsters like beards, irony, and making their own pickles. Environmentalists are liberal and uptight and may also enjoy making their own (organic, locally sourced) pickles.

We even categorize people according to patterns in their facial features—and the consequences of it can be astounding. For instance, baby-faced people—those who have large eyes; thinner, higher eyebrows; large foreheads; and small chins on a rounded face—are perceived to be more innocent and consequently more trustworthy than mature-faced people. I suppose this isn't surprising, since baby-faced people remind us of babies—beings who are practically synonymous with innocence. The problem, obviously, is that while actual babies are less likely to do intentional harm, there's nothing keeping baby-faced adults from doing so. How does this stereotype affect the odds that these adults will be punished when they do intentional harm?

Researchers examining the results of over five hundred small-claims court cases found that differences in baby-faced-ness had a huge impact on whether the defendant was found guilty. For claims of intentional harm (e.g., a neighbor deliberately crashed a car into another's fence after a heated argument), the most mature-faced defendants had a 92 percent chance of being found guilty, compared with only a 45 percent chance among the most baby-faced. But when it comes to negligent harm (e.g., a neighbor wasn't looking and accidentally backed into the other's fence), the baby-faced were *more* likely to be found guilty (85 percent) than the mature-faced (58 percent).[3] In other words, if someone with a delightfully babyish face, like Jennifer Lawrence, Leonardo DiCaprio, or a young Mark Hamill, ran over your begonias, you'd be likely to think he or she was just distracted by a frolicking puppy or a happy song on the radio. But when Clint Eastwood runs over your begonias, you're pretty sure he's doing it on purpose. We are very comfortable saying that baby-faced people are screwups, but uncomfortable thinking they are deliberately bad. On the other hand, a mature-faced person is capable of malicious deeds, but seems less likely to be a bonehead. Being mature-faced gets you taken seriously, even if you aren't fully trusted. It's a trade-off.

We tend to think of stereotypes as inherently negative, but that's not really the case. Just as baby-faced people appear more trustworthy, Asians are believed to be more skilled in math and science, women are assumed to be more caring and nurturing, and blacks more athletically gifted. The contents of a stereotype can have either positive or negative implications for how you will be seen by others. And the more typical of a particular group you seem to be—the more you match others' ideas of what a member of a group should look, sound, and act like—the more strongly the stereotype will be applied to you.

The reality is, stereotypes can be used to your advantage. And on some level we understand this intuitively, when we dress for success or try to fit in. When I applied for my first real job at Bell Labs while still in college, I went to the interview in a suit with my hair pulled back neatly and a minimum of makeup. I wanted to look like a typical Bell Labs scientist so that the company would assume I had the other stereotypical traits of that particular group: intelligence, seriousness, discipline. If I had gone in looking like a typical college student—wearing a flannel shirt, shorts, and a baseball cap (it was the early 1990s)—I would have activated an entirely different and conflicting stereotype: immaturity and inexperience.

In my case, it was clear which group I wanted to appear to belong to. But there are, unfortunately, instances where navigating these waters isn't so easy—when you want to convey qualities that don't coexist nicely in a single stereotype.

Imagine two candidates being interviewed for a leadership position in your company. Both have strong résumés, but while one seems to be bursting with new and daring ideas, the other comes across as decidedly less creative (though clearly still a smart cookie). Who do you think would get the job? And just as important, who *should*?

The answer to the question of who gets the leadership job is usually the less creative candidate. Why? After all, creativity—the ability to generate new and innovative solutions to problems—is obviously an important attribute for any successful business leader. Research shows that leaders who are more creative are better able to effect positive change in their organizations and to inspire others to follow their lead.[4]

The problem, put simply, is this: our idea of what a typical creative person is like is completely at odds with our idea of a typical effective leader. Creative types like designers, musicians, and writers are (stereotypically) nonconformist and unorthodox—not the sort of people you usually put in charge of large organizations. Effective leaders, it would seem, should provide order, rather than tossing it out the window.

Because we unconsciously assume that someone who is creative can't be a good leader, any evidence of creativity can diminish a candidate's perceived leadership potential. For instance, a study in which fifty-five employees rated the responses of nearly three hundred of their (unidentified) coworkers to a problem-solving task for both creativity (the extent to which their ideas were novel and useful) and as evidence of leadership potential found that creativity and leadership potential were strongly negatively correlated. The more creative the response, the less effective a leader the responder appeared.[5]

In another study, participants were told to generate an answer to the question "What could airlines do to obtain more revenue from passengers?" and pitch their ideas in ten minutes to an evaluator. Half the participants were asked to give creative answers (both novel and useful, e.g., "offer in-flight gambling with other passengers"), while the other half were told to give useful but non-novel answers (e.g., "charge for in-flight meals"). The evaluators, unaware of the different instructions, rated participants who gave creative answers as having significantly less leadership ability.

Even though creativity is a much-admired quality, perhaps more so today than ever before, there is a very clear, unconscious bias against creativity when it comes to deciding who gets to be in the driver's seat, thanks to stereotyping. And because of the bias, organizations, believing they are picking people with clear leadership potential, may inadvertently assign leadership positions to people who lack creativity and will preserve only the status quo, believing they are picking people with clear leadership potential.

The Halo Effect

Do you think that someone who is physically attractive is more likely to also be intelligent, honest, creative, or kind? *Of course not*, you say. *There's no reason for those things to go together.* Well, that's perfectly true—but your cognitive miser sees it differently. The tendency to assume that someone possesses other positive qualities from the presence of a single, powerful positive quality is called the *halo effect*. And, aside from first impressions' resistance to change, the halo effect provides yet another reason why first impressions are so important.

If you are handsome or charming, people will assume you are probably smart and trustworthy, too. And in a kind of reverse-halo (a pitchfork effect, perhaps?), if you are unattractive or charmless, people will assume you are dull and dishonest as well. Perhaps my favorite research example of this pervasive phenomenon is a study conducted a few years after President Ronald Reagan left office. Psychologists asked people to guess what Reagan's grade point average (GPA) was when he was an undergraduate at Eureka College—something the vast majority of people would have no way of actually knowing. The researchers found that the participants who had liked Reagan thought that he had an A average, while those who had disliked him thought he had a C average. And the more strongly they had liked or disliked him, the more certain they were about his GPA. They *knew* it to be true. (Incidentally, he had a C average. That's neither here nor there, but I thought you might be curious.)[6]

Halo effects are strengthened by another largely unconscious process—namely, that holding contradictory views of someone (for instance, believing that John is a good person, while knowing at the same time that John cheats on his taxes) causes a psychological pain called *cognitive dissonance*. When asked to put it into words, people describe it as a kind of nagging discomfort or a state of tension. The only way to resolve the dissonance and get rid of the discomfort is to change one of the conflicting views (i.e., choosing to ignore the fact that John cheats on his taxes, or deciding that he is not a good person). So it's just easier to believe that people who have one positive quality have lots of other ones, because there's no risk of creating dissonance. The engine of your mind keeps running smoothly.

The False-Consensus Effect

There's another simple assumption we unconsciously use to make things easier on ourselves: *Other people think and feel what I think and feel.* It's hard for other people to know what you're thinking or feeling. They have to search for clues in your words and actions, carefully considering them and their context. They have to try to take your perspective, rather than their own. It takes a lot of work to get it right. But a lot of work is the last thing the cognitive miser wants to do.

Psychologists call this tendency to believe that others feel the way we do the *false-consensus effect*, and evidence for it is all around you.[7] Ever wonder why people in minority extremist political groups are always acting as if they speak for "the American people"? It's because they genuinely believe that they do—they assume other people agree with them about how the country should be run, and they don't bother to pay for the polling that would tell them otherwise. Shy people think shyness is more common than it is. People who are prone to depression, or have an optimistic outlook, or sweat easily even on cool days, think that most other people do, too. When it comes to everything from religious views to favorite flavors of ice cream, people assume you see things as they do. Because, why wouldn't you?

We also have a tendency to think our bad habits and flaws are universal—that they are, in fact, quite normal. For example, people who are quick to lose their tempers, who cheat on their taxes (or their spouses), or who smoke, drink, or take drugs overestimate the frequency with which others give in to these temptations, too. *Everybody does it*, we think. *I'm not so different*.

But when it comes to goodness, it's a very different story—because we each tend to believe that we have better values and are generally more honest, kind, and capable than others are. Psychologists call this assumption *false uniqueness*. A great

example of this tendency can be found in the work of Chip
Heath, Stanford University psychologist and author of *Made
to Stick*. He showed that while most of us rank intrinsically
motivating factors—such as skill development—as the most
important to us in our careers, we believe that other people
care primarily about extrinsic motivators, like compensation.
In other words, we believe that when it comes to work we do,
our own values are more noble and authentic than those of our
colleagues.

Heath and his team gave University of Chicago MBAs the
opportunity to rank eight possible career motivations in terms
of their personal importance and then to predict how others
would rank them—specifically, how customer service rep-
resentatives at a specific unit at Citibank would rank them.[8]
Finally, the team asked the Citibank reps themselves to rank
their own motivations.

The MBAs rated "learning new things," "developing
skills," and "feeling good about myself" as their top three
motivators, with "pay" coming in fourth. What did they predict for Citibank reps? That the reps' top three motivators
would all be extrinsic: pay, job security, and benefits. Ironically, the Citibank reps didn't even include pay in their top
four—it came in a distant seventh. They had the same top
three motivators as the MBAs, and their fourth was "accom-
plishing something worthwhile," another intrinsic motivator.
Here's another illuminating way of looking at the results from
this study: the MBAs listed an extrinsic motivator as their
own number one motivator only 22 percent of the time, but
listed it as others' number one motivator roughly 85 percent
of the time. And the cost of this particular assumption of false

uniqueness? A workforce that is routinely undermotivated and misguidedly incentivized.

My favorite example of false uniqueness—the one I've taught in my undergraduate classes for years—comes from a national survey conducted in the 1980s.[9] The respondents were asked whether they themselves obeyed each of the Ten Commandments and were then asked to estimate the percentage of Americans who did the same (table 2-1).

These results are mind-blowing for a number of reasons. (For example, apparently one in ten Americans either have committed a murder or aren't sure if they have.) But what's abundantly clear is that Americans in general have a pretty

TABLE 2-1

Us **versus *them*: how we perceive our own and others' adherence to the Ten Commandments**

Commandment	I do	Others do
Do not curse or use profanity	64%	15%
Go to church, synagogue, or mosque on holy days	64%	22%
Respect your parents	95%	49%
Do not commit murder	91%	71%
If married, do not have a sexual relationship with someone other than your spouse	86%	45%
Do not steal	90%	54%
Do not say things that aren't true about another person	88%	33%
Do not envy the things another person has	76%	23%
Do not covet another person's husband or wife	84%	42%
Worship only the one true God	81%	49%

poor opinion of the morality of their compatriots. There are, if these numbers are correct, only a handful of good men and women adrift in a sea of lying, cheating, envious, false-God-worshipping thieves who curse like truckers at their own parents.

. . .

To summarize, there are some assumptions so universal and automatic that you can count on other people to make them about you (and you can count on people to have no idea that they are doing it):

- You are who people expect you to be, in light of their past experience with you.

- The first impression you give is the "right" one, and it shapes how everything else about you is perceived.

- You are like the other members of groups to which you appear to belong.

- If you have a very positive trait—if you are smart, beautiful, funny, kind, and so forth—you are likely to have other positive traits.

- You share the opinions, feelings, and foibles of the perceiver, but not necessarily his or her ethical standards and abilities.

You are never really starting from scratch with another person, even when you are meeting him or her for the first time. The perceiver's brain is rapidly filling in details about you—many before you have even spoken a word. Knowing this gives you a sense of what you've got going for you and what you might be up against. And the more you can know in advance about your perceiver's likes, dislikes, strengths, and weaknesses, the better equipped you will be to anticipate what's being projected onto you.

You don't have to take all of this passively. For example, you can deliberately emphasize your group memberships or your good qualities, to benefit from positive stereotypes and halo effects. You can take pains to make the best possible impression right out of the gate, to use the primacy effect to your maximum advantage. You can make your opinions and values explicitly known. When you have made the wrong impression or have changed in ways you want the people who know you to notice, you can use strategies that will get them to update their beliefs about you (more on this in chapter 9). But however you choose to use the information, it's essential to start by knowing where you probably stand. And since these assumptions are always in play, they are an integral part of that knowledge.

Fortunately, as wired as we are to jump to half-baked conclusions based on stereotype-riddled first impressions, we are also wired to correct those impressions—when it is worth our while to do so.

Key Takeaways

- Much of the time, we are *cognitive misers*—spending as little of our mental energy as we have to in order to get the job done. So when we try to make sense of other people, we use lots of shortcuts and assumptions.

- The most powerful of these shortcuts is perhaps the *confirmation bias*—put simply, people see what they expect to see.

- Thanks to the *primacy effect*, a perceiver's first impression of you is likely to be a lasting impression and to influence how he or she interprets everything else about you. So, no pressure.

- Perceivers don't (necessarily) use stereotypes because they are horrible bigots. Often, they make these assumptions because the human brain is wired to use information about categories to understand members of those categories—including people. Also, stereotypes work most of their effects unconsciously, so your perceiver can say "I never stereotype!" with a straight face and have no idea that he or she does it all the time.

- Generally speaking, other people will assume you share their opinions and attitudes, but not their abilities and moral character. With respect to the latter, they believe they are more talented and less corruptible than you are. Try not to take it personally.

Chapter 3

The Two Phases of Perceiving People

Already something of a success on Broadway, a young dancer from Omaha, Nebraska, was eager to finally make his big break into film. His initial attempts, however, did not go as well as he had hoped. After viewing his MGM screen test, an associate producer there dismissed him, saying, "You can get dancers like this for seventy-five dollars a week." The dancer's first screen test for RKO Radio Pictures wasn't any better—this time, the report came back: "Can't act. Slightly bald. Also dances." True, he wasn't the handsomest young man to ever try to make it in Hollywood. And he *was* balding, and a trifle too thin.

Fortunately for the young man in question, famed studio executive David O. Selznick, best known for producing *Gone with the Wind*, decided to give him a chance. Selznick had really studied the screen test, giving it his full attention—and saw something the others didn't. "I am uncertain about the man," he wrote, "but I feel, in spite of his enormous ears and bad chin line, that his charm is so tremendous that it comes through even on this wretched test." That charmer, if you haven't guessed it already, was Fred Astaire.[1]

"You can get dancers like this for seventy-five dollars a week"? We're talking about the same man George Balanchine would later call "the most interesting, the most inventive, the most elegant dancer of our times." Mikhail Baryshnikov would call Astaire's dancing "unmatched perfection." "Can't act"? You could have fooled me. Astaire received numerous Emmys and Golden Globes, and an Academy Award nomination for his acting. "Slightly bald"? OK, true—but so what? That didn't stop the American Film Institute from naming him the fifth Greatest Male Star of All Time—right behind Humphrey Bogart (he of no great chin line himself), Cary Grant, Jimmy Stewart, and Marlon Brando.

. . .

Mistakes like those made by Fred Astaire's screen test viewers happen because our perception of other people has two distinct phases. And more often than not, our cognitive miser never lets us past the first—very flawed and biased—phase.

Harvard's Dan Gilbert, whom you may know as the author of *Stumbling on Happiness* or as the host of PBS's *This Emotional Life*, also happens to be a central figure in the study of what he calls *ordinary personology*, the "ways in which ordinary people come to know about each other's temporary states (such as emotions, intentions, and desires) and enduring dispositions (such as beliefs, traits, and abilities)."[2] Gilbert's seminal work with Brett Pelham and Douglas Krull at the University of Texas at Austin in the 1980s provided us with the essential insight that perceiving other people is a two-phase process.[3]

Imagine you observe someone weeping at a funeral. In Phase 1 of perception, you (as the observer) ask yourself, *What is it about this person that is causing him or her to cry?* Weeping, for instance, implies that someone is particularly emotionally sensitive. You aren't actually aware that you are asking (and answering) this question. It happens automatically, below your awareness, and in fractions of a second. It is also relatively effortless and riddled with biases that shape the conclusion you ultimately draw.

In Phase 2 of perception, you engage in correction or *discounting*, by taking into account other factors, like the situation the behavior is occurring in. After all, lots of people cry at funerals, right? So weeping at a funeral, upon further consideration, doesn't really suggest that the person is particularly sensitive—anyone might behave that way under the circumstances.

For those of you who have read Daniel Kahneman's *Thinking, Fast and Slow*, you may have already recognized that Phase 1 of perception is part of what Kahneman calls *System 1*, the mental operations that are automatic, relatively effortless, and (almost) completely out of our awareness and control. It includes our abilities to instantaneously recognize anger in a person's face or voice, to drive a car on familiar roads while carrying on a conversation with a passenger, and to know that 2 + 2 = 4 without having to actually add anything. And it relies on all the assumptions and biases described in chapter 2. System 1 is also always on—you don't even have the option of turning it off.[4]

Phase 2 of perception is part of *System 2*, the mental operations that are complex and effortful, require attention, and are usually done with conscious awareness. System 2 engages when necessary, and only when necessary. It includes our abilities to craft a careful apology to the person we've angered, to drive a car in a foreign country on the opposite side of the road we normally drive on, and to work out problems like $21 \times 53 = x$. System 2 operations do the heavy lifting, when getting something right is hard *and* it really matters.

If we are to get a complete and accurate understanding of someone, Phase 2 processing is absolutely necessary. Unfortunately, Phase 2 is very effortful. It takes some serious mental work to weigh all the possible factors influencing someone's behavior and to try to avoid bias. So we need to be motivated to do it—otherwise, we don't reconsider the snap judgment we reached in Phase 1.

Gilbert and his colleagues illustrated this two-phase process by manipulating the ability of perceivers to enter Phase 2. In their most famous study, they asked female participants to watch seven video clips of a young woman having a discussion with a stranger, ostensibly as a part of a getting-acquainted conversation, and to form an impression of her. Each clip was subtitled to indicate the topic the woman and the stranger were discussing, as there was no sound. In five of the clips, the young woman was visibly anxious and uncomfortable.

Gilbert varied the subtitles, so some of the participants were led to believe that the young woman was discussing anxiety-producing subjects—like hidden secrets, personal failures, embarrassing moments, and sexual fantasies. The others were told that she was discussing more-neutral topics during those clips—great books, best restaurants, and world travel.

Finally, half of the people in each group were kept cognitively busy by being asked to simultaneously memorize the conversation topics. This, the researchers reasoned, should make it much more difficult for the perceivers to enter Phase 2, since Phase 2 processing is effortful and mentally taxing. Having to memorize should leave the perceivers too preoccupied to take into account the situation—discussing stressful or neutral topics—when forming an impression of the young woman.

After viewing the video clips, each participant was asked to rate the extent to which she believed the young woman to be an "anxious person." Figure 3-1 shows that when perceivers were not mentally busy—when they could enter Phase 2— they were able to successfully take the situation into account. So, when the young woman appeared anxious discussing topics that would make anyone anxious, they did not conclude that she was an anxious *person.*

But when perceivers were mentally busy and could therefore only go with their Phase 1 assessment, they rated the young

FIGURE 3-1

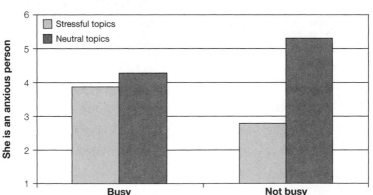

Is she an anxious person?

When they were busy, observers of a woman under stress were less likely to take context into account.

Source: Daniel Gilbert, Brett Pelham, and Douglas Krull.

woman as almost equally anxious regardless of the context. In Phase 1, acting anxious is equivalent to being an anxious person, end of story.

Think about that for a minute, because the implications of these observations are astounding. How often are we mentally busy—preoccupied, multitasking, stressed—when we perceive other people? More to the point, how often are other people mentally busy when they are perceiving *you*? Yes, they are capable of weighing all the factors that may be influencing your behavior under ideal circumstances, assuming they actually know all the factors and are motivated to weigh them. But let's face it, in our everyday lives, circumstances are generally far from ideal, and other people aren't necessarily committed to being right about you. So perception stops at Phase 1 much of the time.

In addition, all of the cognitive biases discussed earlier are setting the stage for bias, even before Phase 1 begins. In this pre–Phase 1 stage, we assign some meaning to the action we're observing—we categorize the behavior in some way. We tend to identify actions in terms of their *intentions*, whenever possible. As a result, we don't think to ourselves, *Frank's fist connected with the side of Bob's face*. We think, *Frank punched Bob*. Even though both statements are equally accurate, *punching* conveys the sense of intent—that Frank was trying to hurt Bob, not accidentally falling into his face with his fist.

I mention this distinction because interpretation—the loss of objectivity—begins with the very act of seeing the behavior itself. Recall the young woman from Gilbert's experiment—the one who was acting anxious in the video clips. She seemed agitated, restless, uncomfortable. She avoided eye contact. People tended to agree that this behavior constituted "anxiousness." But given that women are generally believed to be more emotional than men, and more prone to anxiety, would a *male* target behaving in the same manner have been seen as equally anxious, or might those same signals come across as something more "masculine"—like frustration, impatience, or boredom? Remember that automatic, unconscious biases influence our perception even before Phase 1 begins, directing everything that follows down very different paths.

So you can't really blame people for what they "see" at Phase 1. Well, you can, but you would be blaming them for something they have no awareness of or control over. Which would not be particularly fair, especially since you do it, too.

Hopefully by now it has become obvious that you cannot simply sit back and expect other people to do a better job of judging you accurately. You are going to need to get actively involved.

So let's first take a look now under the hood of Phase 1 perception. You'll learn how it runs entirely on autopilot, how it prefers one kind of explanation for behavior above all others, and how, in light of limited information, it paints a picture of you using the broadest of possible strokes—*traits*.

Phase 1 of Perception

What does it mean for something to be automatic? Psychologists generally agree that for a behavior to count as automatic, four conditions must hold true: (1) the behavior happens without awareness, (2) it occurs without conscious intent, (3) it is relatively effortless, and (4) it is largely, if not completely, uncontrollable. Decades of research show that the operations that occur in a perceiver's brain when he or she is assigning meaning to your behavior and deciding what your behavior says about you meet all four requirements of automaticity.

Perceivers start by assuming that whatever you are doing, it reflects *something about you*—some aspect of your personality, character, or abilities. This, as I mentioned before, is the go-to explanation for all things in Phase 1. Psychologists call this *correspondence bias*—as in, we are biased to see a behavior as corresponding to its actor. Thus, you were late to the meeting because you are not conscientious. Maria lost her temper because she is an angry person. And Alex Trebek knows all the answers on *Jeopardy!* because he's a really smart guy.

Which, of course, might be true, but then again, how much of what you do each day really says something about who you are—about what your personality or character is like? When we look at our own behavior, we perceive that much of what we do each day, the nuts and bolts of living, is more or less what anyone would do under similar circumstances. We are late to meetings because we get caught up in work, lose track of time, or get stuck in traffic. We lose our tempers because something frustrating or stressful has happened, or we've dropped something on our toe. And we'd look smart, too, if we got all the answers to tough trivia questions printed out for us on little cards.*

---

*For years, *Saturday Night Live* did a hilarious spoof of *Jeopardy!*, in which a profoundly hostile and uncooperative "Sean Connery" (played by Darryl Hammond), along with a series of brainless celebrities, tortured Will Ferrell's "Alex Trebek." In one episode, Connery angrily pointed out that Trebek wasn't really so smart, because he "was reading the answers off cards." This was the inspiration for my Trebek example, because at that moment, I remember thinking, "Hang on. I've been making that assumption, too!"

The recognition that correspondence is a bias, rather than an accurate way to draw conclusions about other people's behavior, is, as Gilbert writes, "predicated on the sober insight that most of what people do says very little about them."[5] And that insight is certainly counterintuitive. Frankly it's also more than a little unpleasant to think about. After all, we human beings have a strong desire to see ourselves as both unique individuals and as masters of our own fate. The idea that most of what we do, most of the time, is what *anyone* would do under the same circumstances undermines both our uniqueness and our sense of personal control. It's not surprising, then, that this bias is so pervasive—even though it leads our perception astray.

The most famous example of correspondence bias is perhaps the groundbreaking work of psychologists Edward Jones and Victor Harris.[6] It was 1967, a mere five years after the Cuban missile crisis, and a time when Fidel Castro was a deeply unpopular figure across the United States. Jones and Davis gave groups of college students a short essay to read about Castro. One group was given an essay that argued firmly in favor of Castro and his policies, and the other was given a screed against them. Half of each group was told the essay had been freely written by an anonymous fellow college student, while the other half was told that the instructor had assigned the position the student was to take. After reading the essay, participants in the study were asked to estimate the author's *true* views, on a scale from 0 to 100 (where 0 is a deep hatred and 100 is a profound love of Castro), how much the author personally liked Castro.

In 1967, if I knew nothing at all about your view of Castro, my best bet would be to guess that you didn't like Castro— that was, after all, the norm. So my guess would be on the low end of the scale—perhaps a 20. And logically speaking, if you were required to write an essay advocating a particular viewpoint (something I remember having to do quite a few times in high school), then the fact that you wrote the essay in question would tell me nothing about your actual views. So obviously, I wouldn't use that essay as an indicator of your actual views, right?

Wrong. Chances are I would. As you can see from figure 3-2, participants in the free-choice condition quite logically concluded that freely written pro-Castro essays indicated a liking for Castro (with an average rating around 60), while freely written anti-Castro essays indicated a dislike (with an average just below 20). But here's where it gets strange and disturbing—participants in the no-choice condition still thought pro-Castro essays indicated a liking for Castro (44!). Not as much as freely chosen essays did, but way more than no-choice anti-Castro essays (23).

Again, this is one of those things worth taking a minute to really process. There are all kinds of things each of us has to do each day because we have very little choice. Parents have to leave work when a child gets sick, regardless of how committed they are to their jobs. Managers have to cut positions or pass over for promotion people who deserve it, no matter how devoted the managers are to the members of their team, because of financial constraints or edicts from above. Millions of people who have lost their jobs remain unemployed months—sometimes even years—later,

FIGURE 3-2

Does this essay writer actually like Fidel Castro?

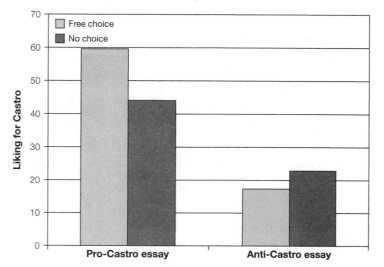

Even when told that the opinion in an essay was assigned, readers assumed it reflected the writer's real feelings about Castro.

Source: Edward Jones and Victor Harris, 1967.

despite doing everything in their power to seek employment. And yet, working parents, particularly working mothers, are routinely perceived as less committed to their careers, managers are frequently blamed for organizational practices that are beyond their control, and the unemployed have a harder time getting hired than someone who already has a job.

In Phase 1, we simply do not consider the situational forces that affect—and sometimes completely control—someone's behavior. We do not take context into account. *That's* correspondence bias.

When you think about it, you begin to realize how little we actually know about other people—how much of our behaviors are driven by context, by common norms and preferences. And how few of our behaviors really say anything about our unique, individual selves. We are much harder to know than we realize or than Phase 1 perception would lead anyone to believe.

Just as people in pre–Phase 1 seem to naturally describe behaviors in terms of a person's intentions (i.e., what the person was trying to do), in Phase 1, we seem to naturally describe people in terms of their *traits*—like smart, funny, creative, dishonest, and introverted. Traits end up playing a big role in our mental representations of one another, too. Chances are good that if I asked you to tell me about your spouse, your boss, or anyone else you know well, you would start rattling off a list of trait terms, rather than talking about their goals, beliefs, hobbies, or the groups to which they belong. Not that you won't do any of the latter—but in general, when psychologists like myself ask people for descriptions of others, traits are what we get.

Of course, as famed psychologist Walter Mischel pointed out long ago, people don't really have traits—if what you mean by *trait* is that people have stable and predictable tendencies to behave in certain ways all the time. Think about it—are extroverts always extroverted? Sure, they may be more gregarious and talkative than others, but probably only in certain situations. Some, for instance, may be extroverted (or clever, funny, warm, or engaging) with their friends, but less so with work colleagues or strangers.

True story: I know a man who met several of his late father's coworkers for the first time at the father's funeral. The son had always known his father to be an introverted, aloof sort of man—one who had barely spoken at home, unless it was to express criticism or complaint. So the son was completely taken aback to learn that his father—according to his colleagues—had been the life of the party, known for his terrific sense of humor and good nature. The son even considered—briefly—asking them if they were sure they had come to the right funeral.

The example is a clear case of someone's displaying two sets of behaviors, associated with different sets of traits, in different settings. Such variability in behavior is the norm, not the exception, as years of research by Mischel and others have shown. A person's "typical" behavior will change as a function of where he or she is, whom the person is with, and what he or she is trying to do. This, of course, is one of the reasons it's relatively easy for two people to have very different impressions of you, depending on the situations they see you in.

The problem with all this Phase 1 thinking in terms of traits, though, is that it leads us to (wrongly) make assumptions we don't even realize we're making and to expect someone's behavior to be more stable and predictable than it ever really is.

In Phase 1, our cognitive miser is running the show. It's content to get the gist of things—to do the bare minimum. And to save itself time and effort, it relies on mental shortcuts and heuristics. These rules of thumb include the biases covered in chapter 2:

> People who are similar to me in one way are probably similar to me in other ways.

> People who have one good quality probably have lots of other ones.

People who are [black, Asian, women, poor, liberal, Muslim, Southern, investment bankers, etc.] are usually [trait].

We almost never even realize we are using assumptions like these to guide our perception, to make sense of someone else's behavior. If I asked you if you even believe any of the above statements to be generally true, you would probably say no. But research shows that people don't need to believe stereotypes and heuristics to use them—because recogniz-ing that a stereotype or some other heuristic is wrong or inappropriate, and therefore shouldn't factor into your view of someone, is really a Phase 2 thing (and we're not there yet). In Phase 1, biases, assumptions, and rules of thumb run the show—influencing the impressions other people make on you in mere fractions of a second.

Of course, the fact that people are unknowingly operating on stereotypes and biases has real costs. Every once in a while a study comes along that illustrates these costs with shocking clarity, and for me one of the most compelling is the work of economists Marianne Bertrand of the University of Chi-cago and Sendhil Mullainathan of Massachusetts Institute of Technology. These researchers sent fake résumés in response to real help-wanted ads that had been posted in Boston and Chicago. They were interested in seeing how variations in the résumés would influence whether the applicant would be called back for an interview. So they manipulated the appli-cant's experience—the better-qualified applicants had more experience, fewer holes in their employment history, and a slightly higher education level. The researchers also varied the names of the applicants to give the impression that the applicant was either probably white (e.g., Emily Walsh and Greg Baker) or probably African American (e.g., Lakisha Washington and Jamal Jones).[7]

After sending out well over a thousand résumés, they discovered that white-sounding applicants received one call back for every ten résumés sent, while African-American-sounding applicants with the same experience received only one call in fifteen. Further analysis revealed that in order for an African American to have the same odds of getting the job as a white applicant, he or she would need an additional *eight years* of experience.

Did the people who screened these applicants knowingly discriminate? Did they think to themselves, *I'd prefer not to hire someone black*? It's tempting to think so—particularly when you are regularly on the receiving end of this sort of discrimination. But the research suggests that in fact, the vast majority of these screeners had no idea that negative stereotypes about blacks—ones the screeners may not even believe—were creeping into their Phase 1 perception and skewing their assessments of the applicants. Biases often act in very subtle ways, altering the way we interpret information without our ever realizing it.

For instance, imagine a résumé showing that the applicant has had three jobs in two years. What does a piece of information like that mean? When Emily Walsh's résumé shows that she's had three jobs in two years, the information is likely to be interpreted more benignly—perhaps as evidence that Emily is trying to find a job that provides the right fit, or even as a sign that she's too hardworking to rest on her laurels. On the other hand, Lakisha Washington's three jobs in two years—thanks to Phase 1 bias from a negative stereotype—is more likely to be seen as indicating a lack of commitment or a poor work ethic.

We can sum this all up with a fairly simple rule. In Phase 1, *the perceivers see what they expect to see*, even when they don't consciously know what they are expecting.

Outrageous? Infuriating? Utterly unfair? Yes, absolutely, all of those things. And the worst part is that it is happening all the time—to every person who is a member of a stigmatized group, to every person who has previously made a bad impression or who has a past he or she would like to leave behind, and to you, too—when perception doesn't get to Phase 2.

Phase 2 of Perception

He had all the outward trappings of an extraordinarily successful man—a penthouse in Manhattan, a yacht, an enviable art collection, prominent philanthropy. His brokerage had offices in New York and London. He flew by private jet to his homes in Montauk, Palm Beach, and Cap d'Antibes, France. A well-respected figure on Wall Street who once served as chairman of the NASDAQ stock exchange, he was also known to treat his employees like family.[8] He was trusted by banks, hedge funds, asset management firms, pension funds, and dozens of charitable institutions to invest billions of dollars of their money.

In fact, his reputation was such that you were considered fortunate if he would even take your money—with his record of providing clients with consistently high returns, he could afford to be selective. One such fortunate client was Elie Wiesel, the Nobel Peace Prize winner and Holocaust survivor. Before investing, Wiesel met with this man over dinner and was so impressed by his philanthropy and his views on ethics and education that he placed all of his own life savings and a third of his charitable foundation's endowment in the man's hands.

This man was, of course, Bernie Madoff—perpetrator of the largest Ponzi scheme in recorded history and almost certainly a profound psychopath. Wiesel, who lost everything he had invested with Madoff, would later call him a "thief, scoundrel, criminal," a "swindler," and "evil"—this from a man who knows something about what evil looks like. And yet, neither Wiesel nor Madoff's other victims saw any trace of these qualities until it was too late.

. . .

One of the most troubling findings in all of psychology has to be the fact that narcissists and psychopaths often make really good first impressions. Phase 2 exists to help the rest of us get past those impressions and learn what other people are actually like.

Generally speaking, in Phase 2, the perceiver wonders whether your behavior might have been caused by something about the situation you are in—something circumstantial, something that would affect others the same way. The person questions his or her own reasoning, trying to detect bias in the conclusions reached. As Gilbert puts it, "the conscious observer trails the parade, cleaning up after the elephants, following, fixing, and occasionally stepping in the conclusions that his mind seems so naturally to produce."*

---

*As a general rule, academic writing is awful—and it's almost never funny (at least, not intentionally). Dan Gilbert is the exception that proves the rule. His chapter on ordinary personology in the *Handbook of Social Psychology* is comprehensive, insightful, and hilarious. If you want to learn more about this topic, see D. T. Gilbert, "Ordinary Personology," in *Handbook of Social Psychology*, vol. 2, ed. S. T. Fiske, D. T. Gilbert, and G. Lindzey (New York: McGraw-Hill, 1998).

Phase 2 is often called the *correction phase*—it's difficult, effortful, and not at all automatic. The perceiver has to have the mental energy, time, and motivation to enter it—if any of those elements are missing, the perceiver will just stick with the impression he or she formed during Phase 1. Often, it takes something really attention-grabbing to push us into it—something like our financial adviser's stealing all our money and then getting indicted. And of course by that time, it's too late.

That's not to say that people never enter Phase 2 *before* disaster happens. Remember the Jones and Harris Castro essay study that revealed the remarkable power of correspondence bias? Years after the study was conducted, Gilbert carefully reviewed it (along with similar studies) and noted that there was often much less agreement among perceivers when essays were assigned as opposed to freely written. While the majority of people stuck with the Phase 1 conclusion ("He wrote an essay praising Castro, so he likes Castro"), at least some of the observers took the situation into account, realizing that an assigned essay is not much of a window into someone's true views. These people had gone into Phase 2—for whatever reason, they were willing and able to weigh all the evidence to judge the writer accurately and fairly.

Unfortunately, we need to consider these admirable perceivers something like the exception that proves the rule. Yes, people can be accurate about you. But usually, they're not.

Most people assume, at least implicitly, that the use of biases to judge other people's behavior is motivated by prejudice. We want to think well or badly of people in a particular group, so we use the stereotype to justify it. But research over the last few decades has shown that humans are simply unable to enter Phase 2 and treat everyone as an individual 100 percent of the time. And some situations are harder than others. For instance, people stereotype more when they are solving complex problems, when they are stressed, when they are in bad moods, and even according to their daily circadian rhythms. Research by psychologist Galen Bodenhausen of the Kellogg School of Management shows that "morning people"— those who feel in top form in the first half of the day —are more likely to use stereotypes in their judgments of others in the afternoon. Those of us who are "evening people," on the other hand, are more likely to use stereotypes right after breakfast.[9]

The work of stereotyping expert Patricia Devine finds that relevant stereotypes about a target tend to be automatically activated in Phase 1, but that in Phase 2 (if you can get there), perceivers can judge the appropriateness of using stereotypes to guide their judgment.[10] Importantly, Devine's work has shown that in Phase 1, stereotypes become activated *even when they aren't endorsed.* In other words, even if I think that stereotypes based on gender, race, or anything else are offensive nonsense, as long as I *know* the stereotype, it will activate in my mind in Phase 1. And as long as a stereotype is active, it can exert influence.

And so, to communicate effectively—to come across the way you intend to in trying to make and maintain good impressions—you will need to really focus on sending the right signals at Phase 1. Getting things right at Phase 1 is by far the easier, and therefore preferable, option. And now that you know the kinds of assumptions perceivers tend to make in Phase 1, you can use that knowledge to your advantage and choose your words and actions accordingly.

But to truly master the art and science of perception, you need to understand that perceivers aren't just trying to form an impression of you. Often, they have an agenda. They are trying to figure out whether they can trust you. Or they are trying to maintain their position of power or their self-esteem. Each of these agendas warps perception in its own unique way, creating a kind of lens through which you are seen. If you understand how the major lenses of trust, power, and ego warp Phase 1 perception, you have an even better chance of coming across as you'd like to. Part II helps you understand these lenses.

Key Takeaways

Phase 1 of Perception

- Perceivers attribute your behavior to something about you—your personality, your abilities, your moral character, your traits—rather than the wider context. This is called *correspondence bias*.

- Perceivers make automatic, effortless assumptions on the basis of your behavior. They use shortcuts and heuristics (like stereotypes) to make sense of you. They are entirely unaware of this process, which can be riddled with all sorts of bias. But because it is all unconscious, they believe they are seeing you objectively as you are.

Phase 2 of Perception

- Perceivers take the situation and other factors into account and revise their impression of you accordingly—making it generally much more accurate.

- Perceivers need to be able to pay attention and motivated to put in the effort—otherwise they stick with their Phase 1 conclusions. And since people are often mentally busy and not particularly motivated, much of perception in real life ends up being based on the processes of Phase 1.

Part II

The Lenses That Shape Perception

Chapter 4

The Trust Lens

President George W. Bush and President Vladimir Putin of Russia emerged from a nearly two-hour private meeting early in Bush's first term pledging that they would work together to keep peace and to usher in a new era of US-Russian relations. "I looked the man in the eye," Bush said as the two stood together at the medieval Brdo Castle, the site of their meeting. "I found him to be very straightforward and trustworthy. We had a very good dialogue. I was able to get a sense of his soul; a man deeply committed to his country and the best interests of his country."

"Can I trust him? I can."[1]

. . .

What President Bush had done in that first encounter with his fellow head of state (though I leave it to the reader to decide whether Bush had done it well) was something that all human beings do when getting to know one another—he looked at Putin through the *trust lens*. This is the lens that people are wearing when they are meeting you for the first time or when they feel they are still getting to know you. Its roots lie in humans' distant past, when determining whether another creature meant you harm was priority number one, all day, every day. In the modern era, we worry less about our physical safety (though we do still worry about that, too) and more about whether new acquaintances are trustworthy.

In other words, we want to know if other people pose a threat to us—to our relationships, to our careers, to our overall happiness and well-being. *Are you going to make trouble for me?* we wonder. We want to know if our new colleague will be competitive and undermine us at work. We want to know if the new couple next door will be friendly and responsible, or if they'll throw loud parties at all hours or constantly complain about the hedges that need clipping. *Is it OK to let my guard down, or do I need to stay on the alert?* When someone else is meeting you—whether or not they realize it consciously—that's what they are wondering, too.

The benefits of projecting trustworthiness (and the costs of failing to do so) are enormous, particularly in the workplace. Studies show, for instance, that the willingness to share knowledge with colleagues—a sticking point in most large organizations—is strongly predicted by feelings of trust among employees.[2] People are less territorial and less concerned with watching their backs when coworkers are identified as friends rather than foes. Organizations whose CEOs and top management teams inspire trust also have significantly lower employee turnover.[3] And employees who trust one another experience greater job satisfaction and less job stress.[4] All these observations are not surprising, really—what's more stressful than having to constantly be on the lookout for coworker sabotage?

And remember those challenging "stretch" goals that everyone is always telling you to set for yourself and your team? Well, recent research shows that while setting higher, more difficult goals does indeed lead to better performance in organizations, it does so only when employees trust the manager doing the goal setting.[5] When that doesn't happen—when your employees aren't confident that you have their best interests (and the organization's) at heart—then no one feels motivated to tackle the big challenges, and stretch goals simply don't get met.

So there is a lot riding on whether you come across as trustworthy. Studies suggest that in order to figure out whether you are trustworthy, others analyze your words and deeds to find the answers to two questions:

1. Do you have good intentions toward me—are you a friend or a foe?

2. Do you have what it takes to act on those intentions?

The second question is just as important as the first, because if the answer to the second one is no, then you are more or less harmless no matter what your intentions are.

Again, other people don't necessarily realize that they are asking (and answering) these questions, because much of this is happening very quickly at an unconscious level. It's a Phase 1 process, though as I described it earlier, it's Phase 1 with a specific agenda. The goal is not simply to form an impression of you, but also to establish whether you are an ally or an enemy.

So where do perceivers find the answers to these questions? Decades of research show that they are highly tuned into two particular aspects of your character, right from the get-go—your *warmth* and your *competence*.[6] Your warmth—friendliness, loyalty, empathy—is taken as evidence that you have good intentions toward the perceiver. Your competence—intelligence, skill, effectiveness—is taken as evidence that you can act on your intentions if you want to. Competent people are therefore valuable allies or potent enemies. Less competent people are objects of compassion or scorn—if we bother to think about them at all.

According to Harvard psychologist Amy Cuddy, a major contributor to this body of research, perceptions of warmth and competence account for roughly 90 percent of the variability in whether you are perceived positively or negatively by others.[7] Thus, the importance of learning to *project* warmth and competence—to come across as a valuable ally—cannot be overstated.

Conveying Warmth

How can you let people know that they can trust you to be on their side—that you want nothing but the best for them? Well, I suppose you could just come right out and say it. *My name is Heidi, and I mean you no harm.* But there are very few circumstances in which that would not be profoundly weird. And weirdness isn't a great facilitator of trust.

Instead, you need to signal your warmth more indirectly. When people try to appear warm, they often do things like give compliments, perform favors, and show interest in the perceiver's thoughts and feelings.[8] They try to display qualities like kindness, sincerity, empathy, and friendliness, each of which captures some aspect of valuing others at least as much as, if not more than, you value yourself.

Let's look at several strategies to improve your warmth quotient.

Pay Attention

When you are with another person, make eye contact and hold it—both when you are speaking and when you are listening. Nod from time to time to show that you are understanding what's being said to you. Smile, especially when the other person does. And above all else, really focus on what is being said to you—people need to feel that they have been heard, even when you can't give them what they are asking for or can't be of particular help. Research shows that eye contact, nodding, and smiling are the three key physical indicators of warmth. Research also shows that people generally have no idea when they are *not* doing these things, so you might want to ask your friends and family if this is something you need to work on.[9]

When a friend of mine began his new position as the head of an editorial team, he deliberately sought to convey to his new employees the sense that he valued everyone's point of view. So at team meetings, he made sure to put on what he calls his "active listening face" while others were speaking. After a few weeks of meetings, one team member finally summoned up the courage to ask him the question that had been on everyone's mind.

"Tim," the employee asked, "are you angry with us right now?"

"No, no," he replied. "This is my active listening face."

"Oh. Well, just so you know, your active listening face looks really angry."

Keep this cautionary tale in mind, and get some feedback on what exactly you are doing with your own face when you are with other people. The answers may surprise you.

Show Empathy

When you are getting to know someone, take the time to mentally put yourself in your perceiver's shoes, to really try to grasp his or her perspective. The more deliberately and vividly you do this, the better. (Don't worry—perspective taking is a skill that gets easier and more automatic with practice.) Try to relate to the perceiver by finding commonalities—shared likes, dislikes, and past experiences. Use phrases like "I imagine you must have felt . . ." to convey that empathy directly.

One particularly effective, but often overlooked, method is what psychologists call the *superfluous apology*—saying "I'm sorry," not as a way of accepting blame, but as a way of expressing regret over another person's hardship. (In other words, apologizing for something you clearly didn't cause.) Many people do this intuitively, saying things like "I'm sorry about the rain," or "I'm sorry your plane was delayed," when it's obvious they are in no way responsible for either circumstance. Superfluous apologies are a simple and powerful way to express that you have taken that person's perspective, understand his or her experience, and wish that things had turned out better. And it produces tangible increases in trust—so much, in fact, that people who receive superfluous apologies become much more willing to part with one of their most precious possessions: their cell phones.

Researchers at Harvard Business School and Wharton had a male undergraduate approach sixty-five strangers in a large train station on rainy days and ask to borrow their cell phone. Half the time, he included the superfluous apology "I'm so sorry about the rain!" before asking, "Can I borrow your cell phone?" A remarkable 47 percent of those who received the superfluous apology gave him the cell phone, compared with only 9 percent who did not.[10]

Hang on, you say. Isn't apologizing a sign of weakness? And couldn't a superfluous apology, under the wrong conditions, be confused with actually taking blame? Well, even if it is, that's OK. Recent research shows that people who are willing to take responsibility for their own failures and for the failures of the teams in which they work are perceived to have greater character, more personal integrity, and more positive intentions toward others—all powerful facilitators of trust.[11] So go ahead and say you're sorry. Good things are sure to come from it.

Trust Them First

Human beings have a deeply rooted tendency toward reciprocity. We are naturally inclined to want to do favors, give gifts, and work to promote those who have done these things for us in the past. This is why sales pitches often involve throwing in something "free"—as in buy-one-get-one-free, or act-now-and-receive-a-free-bottle-opener-with-every-Snuggie. People unconsciously encode this free item as a gift that should be returned in kind, say, by buying the product they are trying to sell you.

The same principle of reciprocity holds when it comes to trust. We are more likely to feel we can trust someone who has trusted us first—someone who has been openly cooperative rather than competitive and put others' interests above their own. Obviously this strategy is not without some risk, but again, the payoff is generally well worth the chance you are taking.

You can also try sharing personal (but appropriate!) stories of your past experiences. Allowing yourself to be a bit vulnerable is a great way to project warmth. Talk about your struggles and challenges. Let the perceiver know your fallible, human side. Far from seeing you negatively, the perceiver is likely to feel that this invitation to intimacy indicates that you are on the same team.

Conveying Competence

Being able—through your skills and abilities—to act on your intentions is a key component of trust. Allies are only valuable when they can be trusted to be effective. When your boss doesn't trust you to act on your intentions, you don't get key assignments, promotions, or the latitude to do things your own way and take risks. When your employees don't trust you to make good on your promises, you don't get their best effort or all the information you need from them to make good decisions.

Much of the advice you hear about projecting competence is fairly obvious: highlight your accomplishments and experience, be self-assured, avoid defensiveness. And again, make eye contact. Really, I can't overstate the importance of this simple strategy. Making eye contact while speaking is, in fact, significantly correlated with IQ—and somehow, people seem to know it. Those who make eye contact are consistently judged as more intelligent.[12] While we're at it, easy-to-understand communication, faster speech rate, gesturing, nodding, and upright posture all lead to perceptions of greater competency, too.

Here are a few less obvious, but no less important, strategies you should be using to get your effectiveness across.

(Appear to) Have Willpower

Willpower is almost entirely overlooked by the make-a-good-impression gurus. But if you want other people to believe that you are trustworthy, you should be aware that you may be seriously undermining that belief if you appear to lack self-control. Research shows that people just won't trust you when you seem to have a willpower problem.[13]

If you think about it, this makes a lot of intuitive sense. We trust people because we know that when things get hard, or when it might be tempting for them to put their own interests first, they'll resist temptation and do what's right. And that, as everyone knows, takes self-control.

Studies show that when you publicly engage in behaviors that are indicative of low self-control, your trustworthiness is diminished.[14] In other words, all those things you know you shouldn't do—smoking; overeating; impulsive spending; being lazy, late, disorganized, excessively emotional, or quick-tempered—may be even worse for you than you even realized, because of the collateral damage they are doing to your perceived trustworthiness.

This, fundamentally, is why the public has such a big problem with politicians who cheat on their spouses. Logically, whether or not my president, senator, or congressional representative breaks a private vow made to his or her mate should have nothing to do with the official's ability to successfully execute the responsibilities of office, right? And yet, it gives us pause, I think primarily because cheating—particularly when you are a public figure with everything to lose if you get caught—seems like the kind of impulsive, reckless behavior only someone lacking in self-control would engage in.

So what can you do to make sure your own trustworthiness is not undermined? Well, the best possible solution is obviously to get a handle on your problems and rid yourself of your bad habits once and for all. Maybe knowing that people trust you less because of them will give you the extra bit of motivation you need to tackle the challenge. But even the best possible solution will probably take some time. None of us rids ourselves of bad habits overnight, or with ease. So in the meantime, do what you can to keep your self-control issues private.

Beware of Overconfidence

While most Western leadership advisers extol the virtues of confidence, psychologists know it isn't all it's cracked up to be—and overconfidence is dangerous. It can lead you to be underprepared, to set unrealistic goals, and to generally make bad choices. On top of all that, when your apparent confidence seems to exceed your competence, you are likely to become an object of derision. Who would trust someone who routinely bites off more than he or she can chew? Who would admire or even want such a person as an ally in the first place? Research by Tomas Chamorro-Premuzic, professor of psychology at University College London, finds that overconfident people tend to be unpopular.[15] And given how annoying it is to hear someone talk the talk without walking the walk, that's really not surprising.

If, instead, you convey a more realistic sense of confidence, people will see you more positively. Show some modesty, and you'll also be less likely to threaten the self-esteem of others (see chapter 6). In fact, Chamorro-Premuzic argues that if you exhibit some modesty with respect to your skills and abilities, people will add, on average, 20 to 30 percent to their estimate of your competence. Toot your own horn too much, and they'll subtract the same amount. This may be a particularly useful piece of advice for executives. After all, in his thirty-plus years of studying what makes good organizations great, Jim Collins (*Good to Great* and *Built to Last*) has found that companies with humbler leaders at the helm consistently outperform their flashier competitors.

Adopt a Power Pose

Competence goes hand in hand with power, as it's generally the people with the most ability and skill who rise in status in an organization. In the animal kingdom, the alphas often convey their dominant status through posture. They assume their full height, stick out their chests, and fan their tail feathers, all to take up as much space as possible and establish their powerful presence. The weaker omegas, on the other hand, bow down low, tucking in their limbs and tails and signaling their submission.

Human beings are no different. The most confident, powerful guy in the room is usually the one whose physical movements are most expansive—legs apart, leaning forward, arms spread wide while he gestures. He's the CEO who isn't afraid to swing his feet up onto the conference room table, hands behind his head and elbows jutting outward, confident in his power to spread himself out however he damn well pleases.

The nervous, powerless person holds himself very differently—he makes himself physically as small as possible:

shoulders hunched, feet together, hands in his lap or arms wrapped protectively across his chest. He's the guy in the corner who is hoping he won't be called on, and often is barely noticed.

Psychologists have known for some time that powerful and powerless individuals adopt these poses unconsciously and that the poses themselves are in fact perceived (also unconsciously) by others as indictors of status. Your posture, like it or not, tells people a lot about you.

But more recent research reveals a new, far more surprising relationship between power and posing: their influence works in both directions. In other words, holding powerful poses can actually make you more powerful.

In one study, Amy Cuddy and her colleagues asked male and female participants to hold two poses, each for one minute. The poses were either high power (the CEO feet-up-on-the-table pose with hands behind head; or standing feet apart while leaning over a table, supported by one hand resting on the table) or low power (sitting with shoulders slumped forward and hands in lap; or standing with feet together and arms folded tightly across chest).[16]

After holding the high-power poses, the participants not only reported that they felt significantly more "powerful" and "in charge," but were also more willing to take a risk when offered the chance to gamble their study earnings for double the money. The high-power posers also experienced significant increases in testosterone and decreases in cortisol (measured in their saliva), a neuroendocrine profile that has been linked in past research to dominance, competitiveness, adaptive responding to challenges, disease resistance, and leadership ability. So not only did high-power posing create psychological and behavioral changes typically associated with powerful people, but it also created physiological changes characteristic of the powerful as well.

Low-power posers, on the other hand, experienced significant drops in testosterone and increases in cortisol—giving them the typical physiological profile of the nervous and risk-averse omega. The pose left them feeling less powerful and less willing to take a chance on a big win.

How you are sitting, right now? Reflect on what you are typically doing with your body when you are at your desk, in a meeting, or simply socializing. What message is your body language—your posture, your stance, your gesturing—sending to everyone in the room? And just as important, what message is it sending to your own brain? If you sit all curled up in a ball or stand with your arms wrapped around your chest like battle armor, you are going to end up looking and feeling less powerful and less competent because your brain will assume that *that's what you are*. Adopting a high-power pose is a great way to subtly signal your competence—especially if you aren't the type to sing your own praises—while simultaneously providing a power boost to help you tackle your next challenge.

Emphasize Your Potential

It would be reasonable to assume that the best way to project competence would be to focus others on your history of accomplishments. After all, a person's track record of success is the single most important factor in determining whether he or she gets hired for a job. Or is it?

As it happens, it isn't. When we are deciding whom to hire, promote, or do business with, it turns out that we aren't as impressed by the "big thing" nearly as much as we are by the "next big thing." We have a yet another unconscious bias, leading us to prefer the potential for greatness over someone who has already achieved it.

A set of ingenious studies conducted by Stanford's Zakary Tormala and Jayson Jia and Harvard Business School's Michael Norton paints a very clear picture of our unconscious preference for potential over actual success.[17] In one study, Tormala, Jia, and Norton asked participants to play the role of an NBA team manager who had the option of offering a contract to a particular player. To evaluate the player, the participants were given five years of excellent statistics (points scored, rebounds, assists, etc.). These statistics were described either as ones that the player had actually earned in five years of professional play or as projections of how he was capable of playing (i.e., his potential) in his first five years.

Then the "managers" were asked, "What would you pay him in his sixth year?" Those who had evaluated the player with potential for greatness said they would pay him nearly a million dollars more in annual salary ($5.25 versus $4.26 million) than those who evaluated the player with a record of actual greatness. Potential evaluators also believed their player would score more and would be more likely to make the All-Star team.

The researchers found the same pattern in evaluations of job candidates. In this case, they compared perceptions of someone with two years of relevant experience who had scored highly on a test of leadership achievement and someone with no relevant experience who scored highly on a test of leadership potential. (Both candidates had equally impressive backgrounds in every other way.) Evaluators believed the candidate with leadership potential would be more successful at the new company than the candidate with a proven record of leadership ability.

In other studies, the researchers showed how we prefer artwork and artists with potential to win awards over those that actually have, and prefer restaurants and chefs with the potential to be the next big thing in dining over those that have already made their name. In a particularly clever study, they compared two versions of Facebook ads for a real stand-up comedian. In the first version, critics said "he is the next big thing" and "everybody's talking about him." In the second version, critics said he *"could be* the next big thing" and that "in a year, everybody could be talking about him." The ad that focused on his potential got significantly more clicks and likes.

And this is not, incidentally, a pro-youth bias in disguise. It's true that the person with potential, rather than a proven record, is sometimes also the younger candidate, but the researchers were careful to control for age in their studies and found that it wasn't a factor.

So, since preferring potential over a proven record is both risky and inherently irrational, why do we do it? According to these findings, the potential for success, as opposed to actual success, is more interesting because it is less certain. When human brains come across uncertainty, they tend to pay attention to information more because they want to figure it out, which leads to longer and more in-depth processing. High-potential candidates make us think harder than proven ones do. As long as the information available about the high-potential candidate is favorable, all this extra processing can lead (unconsciously) to an overall more positive view of the candidate's competence. (That part about the information available being favorable is important. In another study, when the candidate was described as having great potential, but there was little evidence to back that up, people liked him far less than the proven achiever.)

All this suggests that you need a very different approach to projecting competence than the one you intuitively take, because your intuition is probably wrong. People are much more impressed, whether they realize it or not, by your potential than by your track record. It would be wise to start focusing your pitch on your future, rather than on your past—even if that past is very impressive indeed. It's what you *could* be that makes people sit up and take notice.

Conveying Warmth and Competence: The Paradox

Here comes the tricky part. You may have begun to notice that the patterns of behaviors we associate with warmth and competence often directly contradict one another. In other words, if you appear too warm, people may question your competence— and if you appear too competent, people may assume you're cold.

Think about it. When people are trying to appear warm, they are agreeable, engage in flattery, make kind gestures, and encourage others to talk (i.e., they are good listeners). But when they want to appear competent, they do the opposite— speaking rather than listening, focusing the conversation on their own accomplishments and abilities, and challenging the opinions of others as a demonstration of their own expertise.[18] In fact, both consciously and unconsciously, people tend to use this knowledge and play down their competence (i.e., play dumb) to appear warm, and vice versa.

Psychologists refer to the apparent contradiction that people see in these traits as the *compensation effect*. You see evidence of this effect in some stereotypes—that women are warmer but less competent than men, that rich people are intelligent but relatively cold. Career women feminists, female intellectuals, and lesbians—so-called nontraditional women—are seen as more competent, but also (perhaps consequently) less warm. Sexism toward these women can take a particularly hostile form, in part because of their perceived failure to adhere to the women-are-warm-but-less-competent norm.

Research by Cuddy, Fiske, and Peter Glick reveals yet another troubling result of these beliefs in the modern workplace: working mothers seem warmer but less competent than other employees, while the perception of working dads gains warmth *without* losing competence.[19] Talk about unfair! In fact, so powerful are these beliefs that when given only one kind of information (e.g., person A is very friendly, or group A is very warm), perceivers will fill in the blanks, assuming that the person or group is probably also less competent than a low-warmth individual or group.[20]

It seems, on the surface, to be a damned-if-you-do, damned-if-you-don't kind of scenario. If you're seen as warm but not competent, you elicit compassion but a lack of respect. If you appear competent but cold, you elicit respect but also envy and wariness. And don't be surprised if your colleagues are only too happy to see you stumble.

Fortunately, there is a way to resolve this paradox: focus on projecting those qualities of warmth that do not appear to evoke low competence—the *moral* aspects of warmth. Research by Paul Rozin (the psychologist who convinced me to abandon my chemistry major for a career in psychology, God bless him) and his colleagues has argued that moral character, rather than overall warmth, is really the best predictor of whether someone will act on his or her good intentions toward you, and therefore is the better indicator of whom to trust.

They found that traits like *courageous, fair, principled, responsible, honest*, and *loyal*—traits that lack the touchy-feeliness we generally associate with warmth—convey good intentions and trustworthiness even better than traits like *sociable, funny*, and *agreeable*, and without the connotations of low competence. (Of course, *sociable, funny*, and *agreeable* have the advantage of being much easier to convey, particularly in a short time. In a brief conversation, someone is unlikely to come away thinking you are *principled*, for instance.)

Importantly, warmth does not have to mean "huggable," "nurturing," or "kind of guy I'd like to have a beer with." So if you just aren't the warm-and-fuzzy type, and maybe talking about feelings makes you uncomfortable, fear not. You can project your good intentions and navigate the perils of the trust lens by being someone the perceiver can always count on to do the right thing. After all, this is ultimately what trust is actually about.

Trust and Leadership

Trust is obviously essential to good leadership. When your team members trust you as a leader, they increase their commitment to team goals. Communication improves—ideas flow more freely, increasing creativity and productivity. Perhaps most important, in the hands of a trusted leader, employees are more comfortable with change and more willing to embrace a new vision. When your team doesn't trust you, you don't get the group's best effort or all the information you need from your team members to make good decisions. And you find yourself unable to inspire, unable to influence, and unable to create real change.

So we can all agree that trust is good. The problem, however, is that most people see leadership as being first and foremost about competence—as about strength and confidence and accomplishments. We are so eager to prove that we know what we're doing as leaders that we neglect the arguably more important part of the trust formula: proving that we will act with others' interests in mind. In other words, warmth is an afterthought.

Cuddy's research shows that when you project competence *before* warmth, you run the risk of appearing cold . . . and eliciting fear from your employees. They might respect you, but fearful employees are rarely able to work at their best. And you certainly can't blame them for wanting to jump ship once an offer to work for someone who doesn't make them constantly anxious comes along.

So, are you a leader who projects warmth first—a leader whose top priority is making sure your team members feel they can trust you? If you suspect the answer might be no, you need to start working on your warmth pronto, because you will never be trusted without it.

Key Takeaways

- The very first thing another person will seek to determine about you is whether he or she can trust you—in broad strokes, whether you are a friend or foe.

- The decision to trust is made almost entirely unconsciously and is based on the extent to which you project *warmth* and *competence*. Warmth is a signal that you have good intentions toward your perceiver; competence signals that you are capable of acting on those intentions.

- Convey warmth by paying attention—make eye contact and hold it, smile, nod to indicate understanding. Show empathy and concern, when appropriate. Above all, be fair and be true to your word. And be willing to trust first, when necessary, to put the other person at ease.

- Convey competence by making eye contact (yes, it's good for competence, too) and sitting up straight. Don't advertise your personal demons. Don't sell yourself short, but don't brag either—a little bit of modesty goes a long way to impressing others. And when you aren't feeling particularly competent, adopt a *power pose*.

- Leaders should always be careful to prioritize warmth, not competence, when trying to inspire trust and loyalty.

Chapter 5

The Power Lens

There's a passage by English humorist Douglas Adams that always comes to mind when I think about the power lens. In *Dirk Gently's Holistic Detective Agency*, Adams writes about horses:

> *They have always understood a great deal more than they let on. It is difficult to be sat on all day, every day, by some other creature, without forming an opinion about them.*
>
> *On the other hand, it is perfectly possible to sit all day, every day, on top of another creature and not have the slightest thought about them whatsoever.*[1]

What Adams correctly noted, with his characteristic insightfulness and humor, is that power changes how we see one another—assuming we see one another at all.

Just as the trust lens is worn when perceivers are still determining whether you are friend or foe, the power lens is worn whenever there is a disparity of power—specifically, when the perceiver you are interacting with has relatively *more* power than you do. And this lens has a straightforward agenda: prove yourself useful to me, or get out of my way.

Also like the trust lens, the power lens distorts Phase 1 perception for the person with power. Unlike the trust lens, though, it doesn't affect all of us all the time—in any given situation, the relatively powerless are unaffected.

This means that while having more power can warp your view of the less powerful, having less power rarely distorts your view of the more powerful. Oh sure, maybe the less powerful are occasionally fearful—or envious—of the powerful. But being powerless makes people much more motivated to be accurate—to engage in Phase 2 perception and take nothing for granted. Those with less power need to be able to predict how those with more power will think, feel, and act—because the less powerful depend on the more powerful to get what they want.

When I talk about power, I don't necessarily mean CEOs, government leaders, or the rich and influential—although those people undoubtedly wield power. I also mean it much more broadly, to include the kind of garden-variety power that ordinary people encounter or experience on a daily basis. Perhaps the most commonly agreed-upon—though decidedly technical—definition of power among psychologists is this: power is *asymmetrical control over desired resources.*[2] In other words, powerful people get to make the decisions, and power-less people get to live with the results.

Here's another way of looking at it: Imagine two friends, Amy and Claire. Amy needs to borrow five hundred dollars from Claire to hold her over until her next payday. Now, Claire can be said to have power over Amy, because Amy depends on Claire to get something that she wants—something she can't get without Claire's cooperation. Amy's (temporary) dependence on Claire, in turn, gives Claire the ability to determine Amy's outcomes (i.e., giving her the loan or not) and to make demands on Amy in exchange for a better outcome (*How about you help me move to my new apartment on Saturday, then?*).

Thought about this way, power can clearly have many sources. Managers have more power than their employees, because managers control important outcomes—everything from task assignments and parking spaces to whether you even have a job in the first place. Popularity is a kind of power, too, since popular people are the gatekeepers to the most coveted circles of society. Their friendship, in this case, is the desired resource in question. And popular people get to dictate the norms of style, speech, and behavior that the unpopular must follow if the latter are to have any hope of fitting in. Wealthier people enjoy more power than the poor, because the affluent depend less on others to obtain the things they desire. And experts, like scientists, celebrity endorsers, editorialists, and critics, have power—the power to influence public opinion.

What is really essential to understand about all of these sources of power is that they are all dependent on context and circumstance. Your boss only has power over you if you want to continue working for him or her—once you've decided to quit, the boss's power evaporates. (If your boss then decides to beg you to stay, suddenly you are the one with the power to make demands in exchange for the outcome he or she wants. Got to love it when that happens.)

The point is that power dynamics are not simple or static. It's really never that person X is more powerful than you, period. It's that person X is more powerful under these specific circumstances, with respect to these particular issues, at this point in time. And that is when he or she will be wearing the power lens.

How Power Changes People

Being in a position of power relative to those around you certainly does change you—not necessarily in an evil way, but there is a definite shift in how you see things when you are in the driver's seat. Let's start with the good news.

The Good

When people feel relatively powerless, they are concerned primarily with safety and security—with hanging on to what they've already got. They have their guards up and have to stay focused on not making mistakes or displeasing the higher-ups. As a result, their thinking is more concrete, more conventional, and more risk-averse.

When people feel powerful, on the other hand, they tend to think in more abstract, big-picture ways—the kind of thinking that is consistently associated with creativity and innovative problem-solving. Power also increases optimism and self-assurance, both of which allow us to embrace risk and tackle tough challenges.

In fact, research shows that on average, feelings of power lead to better performance, particularly on complex or difficult tasks that require effort and persistence. This is true for four reasons:

- **Powerful people feel responsible** to those they have power over (i.e., the group they are leading). This is an added motivation that the relatively powerless often lack, and it makes throwing in the towel a less attractive option.

- **All eyes are on them.** Powerful people—particularly leaders—feel more individually identifiable, which increases their sense of accountability. Because they expect to be noticed by others, they feel pressured to perform well and set a good example for others.

- **Power stimulates the brain,** specifically, what psychologists refer to as the brain's *executive function*, located in the prefrontal cortex (the part of your brain right behind your forehead). These processes are instrumental when it comes to setting and achieving goals. For example, when participants in laboratory experiments are given power over the outcomes of others (usually their fellow students), they are better able to control their attention, effectively plan future behavior, and take goal-directed actions, all hallmarks of superior executive function.

- **Power keeps you going.** Research shows that powerful people not only outperform the less powerful, but also continue to do so even when their energy and willpower have been seriously depleted. As I mentioned before, self-control is a limited resource—like a muscle in your body, it gets tired when you've given it a good workout. Typically, when you've depleted your self-control by working on something really challenging, your performance on subsequent tasks suffers. Powerful people, however, are slower to show signs of depletion—they can keep up their A-game longer, thanks in part to their strong motivation and heightened executive functioning.

The Sometimes Good, Sometimes Bad

Thanks to all that optimism and confidence, feeling powerful can lead someone to engage in riskier behavior than he or she otherwise would. And risk, as you know, can be either good or bad. "Nothing ventured, nothing gained" and "Fools rush in . . ." seem to apply to the powerful in equal measure.

In a series of studies, Columbia Business School's Adam Galinsky and his colleagues showed that when male and female participants felt powerful, they preferred riskier business plans (with bigger potential rewards) to more-conservative plans. Moreover they divulged more information and were more trusting during negotiations, chose to "hit" more often during a game of blackjack, and indicated they were more likely to engage in unprotected sex during a one-night stand.[3] Except for that last one, these tendencies to go for the riskier option might prove beneficial, but if you aren't a particularly good judge of when to take a risk, power can get you into big trouble.

When in power, people focus more on the potential payoffs of their risky behavior and much less (if at all) on the possible dangers. They are even overly optimistic about things no one could possibly control. For instance, compared with the relatively powerless, they believe they are less likely to encounter turbulence on an airplane or to run into a dangerous snake while on vacation. (Logically it follows that they are probably not worried about snakes *on* a plane, either, but Galinsky didn't test that combination.)

The Ugly

This may come as no surprise, but powerful people are more likely to act like selfish jerks. Research by a group of Berkeley researchers, led by Paul Piff, has found evidence of power-induced jerkiness in even the most mundane daily activities. In one of their studies, the researchers observed drivers at a busy four-way stop sign and used the make and model of car as a way of estimating the driver's social class and wealth. The highest-status cars—the Mercedes, BMWs, and Porsches— cut off other drivers (by going before it was their turn) 30 percent of the time, compared with only 7 percent for the lowest-status cars. In a second study, where researchers were stationed at a clearly marked crosswalk, high-status cars failed to yield to a pedestrian trying to cross nearly 50 percent of the time, while lower-status cars failed to yield only 25 percent of the time. (Interestingly, the very lowest-status cars—your beat-up, rusty, rag-for-a-gas-cap type cars—stopped for pedestrians *every* time.)[4]

Other studies by Piff and his colleagues showed that people with relatively high status were more likely to tell lies or cheat on a friendly game. And in my absolute favorite of these studies, the researchers gave college students—who saw themselves as having relatively high or low socioeconomic status— a packet of questionnaires to complete on a variety of topics. When the students had finished, the experimenter took out a jar of individually wrapped candies and explained that while these candies were meant for the young children who were currently in a study down the hall, "You can have some if you want." So, who *literally* takes the most candy from children?

You guessed it! The richer participants took roughly twice as much candy as the poorer participants.

So what is it, exactly, that makes these people more likely to behave unethically? Piff argues that those with higher socioeconomic status are somewhat dehumanized by their experience of wealth and power. Because they depend less on others to get what they want, they become more self-focused, less aware of those around them, and less likely to experience empathy. And interesting evidence from functional MRI studies of brain activity pinpoints how these differences play out on a neural level.

Motor resonance is the term neuroscientists use to describe a fascinating phenomenon: when you watch another person doing something—giving a speech, cooking a meal, dancing a jig—the same neural circuitry that would be involved if you were speaking or cooking or dancing becomes activated, as if you were the actor, rather than simply the observer. Motor resonance provides a means of understanding the actions of others and of imagining things from their perspective. Interestingly, and perhaps not surprisingly at this point, people who feel powerful show significantly less motor resonance when observing others than the relatively powerless do.[5] This incredible, sophisticated brain architecture—one that has evolved to give us unique access to the thoughts and feelings of our fellow human beings—just sits there, doing nothing. Because to your cognitive miser, the gist is fine.

In the end, this is the biggest obstacle you deal with when you deal with the powerful. It's not so much that they think they are better than you as it is that they simply do not think about you at all.

Here's the really scary thing: power does the same thing to you. Even if you only feel powerful momentarily.

Just about every research finding I've described so far in the chapter is obtained not only when participants have a generally higher sense of power, but also when they were momentarily made to feel powerful in the experiment. And that part is really important, because when we witness instances of bad behavior among the rich and powerful, it's easy to assume that the kind of people who seek power are also the kind of people who take crazy risks and behave irresponsibly and unethically. What the research of Galinsky, Piff, and others suggests is that power itself is the driving force—and that even someone who is new to power will be prone to the same kinds of mistakes as someone who has enjoyed a lifetime of it.

And remember how power is generally associated with superior performance? I should probably explain why—or more specifically, when—it's not. You see, powerful people often have a lot on their plates, and it stands to reason that they can't possibly bring their best to everything. They need to decide where to put their effort and where to hold back. So, how do they decide?

The short and unsurprising answer is that people with power generally withhold effort when they feel that the task in question is unworthy of a powerful person—in other words, when it seems like the kind of thing an underling would do. This attitude can and does affect performance. For example, in the research by Galinsky I referred to earlier, when participants were given boring, repetitive tasks like filling out multiplication tables, those assigned to a leadership role (i.e., those given power) performed worse than nonleaders and complained that they didn't think it was the sort of task a leader should have to do.

Arrogant as this may seem at times, you have to admit that this attitude makes some sense. Powerful people approach tasks with greater energy and intensity, but their well of energy and intensity isn't bottomless. They need to be selective—to be motivated tacticians. Which is why powerful perceivers often choose to spend elsewhere the energy they could be spending on getting an accurate impression of *you*.

How the (Relatively) Powerful See You

What we know for certain is that powerful perceivers often rely heavily on the cognitive miser's bag of shortcuts to keep the time and energy they must devote to perceiving you to the bare minimum. There is less agreement on why that's true, however. Some argue that it's purely about *cognitive load*— that the powerful want to conserve their mental resources for the really important stuff (or, more accurately, for what they believe to be the really important stuff). Some say it's more of an accidental consequence of the self-focus that power tends to create. Other researchers point to evidence that suggests the powerful want (largely unconsciously) to maintain a sense of *psychological distance* from the less powerful and thus deliberately pay less attention to them.

There's good reason to believe that all three of these factors are playing a role in the functioning of the power lens. Here's what the power lens is doing: powerful people seem to feel that they need not have complex, nuanced views of you if you are (relatively) powerless. As a consequence, the Phase 1 tendency to stick with any assumptions they have about you is intensified. An abundance of studies have reliably shown that feeling powerful tends to make ordinary people more stereotypic in their thinking, too.[6]

Research shows that feelings of power will make an interviewer or a supervisor more likely to be biased by stereotypic information when the person is choosing job candidates or distributing rewards. He or she is likely to be particularly biased by the negative stereotypes about the target (women are too emotional, bad at math, etc.)—though the evaluator will likely have no idea that the bias is influencing his or her judgment.[7] (And yes, even a female interviewer or supervisor will, unconsciously, use negative stereotypes of women to judge other women. One of the most interesting, if a bit horrifying, discoveries in the past twenty years of social psychology has been that people can be influenced by stereotypes even when they believe them to be utterly wrong.)

When powerful people experience feelings of threat—when, say, the source of their power is illegitimate or unstable—they often negatively stereotype subordinates even more. For instance, a set of studies found that people assigned to be group leader paid particular attention to negative stereotypic information about their other group members, but only when these leaders were *randomly* chosen to be group leaders. When, instead, they felt they had earned the role through an evaluation of their social skills and suitability for the job, the bias disappeared.[8] Research like this suggests that powerful leaders can and do use negative stereotyping strategically, to bolster their sense of entitlement to power.

But the powerful are not always less perceptive. There are circumstances when power leads to enhanced, more accurate perception. And therein lies the key to mastering the power lens.

Research by psychologists Jennifer Overbeck and Bernadette Park has shown that powerful perceivers aren't uniformly terrible—in fact, the researchers argue, it would be more accurate to describe the perceivers as *flexible*, using their attention as a resource that they deploy strategically. In other words, when their goal requires them to pay close attention to individuating information about a person to form a more accurate impression of him or her, powerful people do so more effectively than the relatively powerless.

In one of Overbeck and Park's studies, for example, participants were assigned the high-power role of supervisor in a publishing company. Their job was to manage five telecommuting proofreaders, who were actually confederates in the experiment. These confederates would report on their own progress—the number and nature of the errors they had found and the problems they were encountering. Each proofreader was also assigned a personality profile that he or she tried to express in various ways in the reports. "Joe" was good-natured and friendly, "Sally" was smart and efficient, and so on.

The supervisors were given one of two goals:

Goal 1: Make your workers feel engaged and included.

*Your task is to establish an atmosphere in which workers
feel positive, engaged, and with a sense of belonging
to the organization. It has been demonstrated that this*

atmosphere causes workers to be more enthusiastic and motivated to focus on doing what is best for the company. If the right environment is established, the rest of the company's goals can be met with much less effort and difficulty. Workers are more likely to channel their effort to the company's benefit, by doing their work rather than (for example) watching TV while they are at home, which is basically taking pay without working. Use whatever means you can derive to accomplish this goal, including the kinds of recommendations and feedback you provide, and decisions about workers' pay.

Goal 2: Make your workers more productive and efficient.

Your task is to get the workers performing at the goal level by the end of the work session. In order for telecommuting to be a viable option, it is critical that people perform as productively and efficiently as possible. Therefore, we need to discover whether we can assure the necessary levels of production. We do not want workers sabotaging the company's goals by sitting at home watching TV when they should be working. Use whatever means you can derive to accomplish this goal, including the kinds of recommendations and feedback you provide, and decisions about workers' pay.[9]

Note that establishing feelings of engagement and belonging (goal 1) requires a more nuanced understanding of each employee. Thus, spending time and effort on forming an accurate impression of each employee is more essential for successfully reaching this goal, compared with when the goal is to simply keep all the employees working at a good pace (goal 2).

After receiving their goals, the supervisors communicated with their workers about their reports via computer over the next hour. The supervisors then rated their impressions of each of their workers' performance and personality.

The researchers found than when a power holder was given the goal of making workers feel engaged and included, he or she was indeed much more likely to differentiate between them and to accurately discern their individual characteristics. In other words, powerful people pay will pay attention to you when doing so facilitates their goal. As Overbeck and Park argue, much of the research demonstrating biased perception on the part of the powerful was conducted in contexts in which careful attention was not necessary or rewarded. Which means that to get powerful people to perceive you accurately, you are going to need to make it necessary or rewarding.

How to Be Seen Clearly through the Fog of Power

There is a really important insight in this research. For the powerful, your *instrumentality* is key. Frankly, it is all that matters. What can you do to help powerful people reach *their* goals? How is having an accurate understanding of you in their self-interest? If they invest time and mental energy into really "getting" you, what is the potential return on their investment?

The first step to being instrumental is to understand the desires and challenges of the powerful person in question. Let's say, for the sake of argument, that the powerful person is your direct supervisor. You know what your targets and stretch goals are for the year—what are your boss's? Where does he or she need help the most—and how could you ease this burden? Where is your supervisor falling behind? Most of us have a little wiggle room when it comes to how we allocate our time. By prioritizing your own tasks in such a way that they provide assistance to your boss where he or she needs it most, you can dramatically increase your perceived usefulness.

Also, it goes without saying that to be instrumental, you need to do everything that is directly asked of you—but where you can really stand out is by anticipating your boss's needs, before he or she asks. I had a research assistant who did exactly that— who prepared literature reviews for me that she knew I would eventually need, who had documents ready before I asked for them, who took over, without being asked to, the scheduling of research participants, a thankless and frustrating job. I wrote her the most glowing recommendation I've ever written for a student. And when she left my lab and moved on to graduate school, I was depressed for a week. *That's* instrumentality.

Instrumentality isn't about being nice—it's about being useful. Whenever I'm at a conference or an awards dinner with a few movers and shakers in attendance, I'm always a little amazed to see how reflexively people seem to shower the powerful with flattery and ingratiation. It's so natural, it just seems to come rushing out of their mouths. *I really admire the work you do. I'm such a big fan. Your marketing strategy is brilliant.* Sure, that might elicit a smile. And of course, being warm signals that you are a friend and not a foe, which is good. But believe me when I tell you that powerful people by and large don't give a damn that you think they are awesome. To really get their attention, you'll need to let them know how *you* can help facilitate their continuing, increasing awesomeness. If you want them to see the real you, this is the only way.

That probably sounds a little Machiavellian to you, but in fairness, powerful people tend to be powerful because they have a lot of responsibilities and a whole lot going on. Everyone's mental and emotional resources are limited. It may be arrogant, but it's also fundamentally practical. You have to be worth taking time and energy for, and powerful people have no reason to believe you are unless you give them one.

That does not mean that you should walk up to powerful people and just start listing your good qualities. They don't care about those, either. It's the goals that matter. What are their goals, do they align with yours, and how can you be instrumental in reaching them? Know the answers to these questions, and you'll have *their* power lens working for *you*.

Key Takeaways

- People with (relatively) more power perceive you differently. In large part, this comes from focusing more on achieving their own goals and from being less interested in the concerns and perspectives of others. As a result, they take lots of shortcuts and have less complex, nuanced views of other people.

- Power depends on context—someone with more power than you in a particular point in time, in a specific situation, may have less power in another. Power is dynamic and changing. We take the power lens on and off accordingly.

- Power causes perceivers to rely more heavily on stereotypes and prior expectations. This makes it more difficult for you to distinguish yourself as a unique individual in their eyes.

- High-power perceivers can be accurate, when accuracy is necessary for them to reach their goal. That is why instrumentality is so important—be someone who helps the powerful person achieve his or her goals, and the perceiver will find it worth the time and mental energy to see you for who you really are.

Chapter 6

The Ego Lens

Actress and lifestyle guru Gwyneth Paltrow had a very interesting 2013. She starred in the blockbuster film *Iron Man 3*, released a best-selling cookbook called *It's All Good*, and was voted *People* magazine's "Most Beautiful Person." She was having quite a run of good fortune until, a few weeks after *People*'s results were announced, a new story came to dominate the publicity surrounding her—that she had been voted by readers of *Star Magazine* the "Most Hated Celebrity in Hollywood."

Now, I'm not saying that Paltrow doesn't invite some of the negativity that comes her way by advertising her high-end, healthy-eating, absurdly fit, and all-around superior personal life so publicly through her lifestyle website and newsletter, *Goop*. But are the accusations that she is "preachy," "arrogant," "pretentious," or "elitist" really fair? Comb through a smattering of the anti-Gwyneth rhetoric you find online, and there is very little evidence offered that she is any of those things, save the occasional quote that was probably taken out of context (and almost certainly interpreted as unkindly as possible).

Maybe Gwyneth Paltrow is a real jerk—or maybe she isn't. But an awful lot of people who have never met her seem to be sure that she is. Why?

Most of us assume that the beautiful people have it made—that being attractive gives you all sorts of advantages across the board. Much of the time, we are right. Thanks to the halo effect we covered in chapter 2, when people are attractive, we often unconsciously assume that they have lots of other good qualities, too. We perceive them to be warmer, kinder, smarter, funnier, and more honest, simply because they are easier on the eyes.

There are times, however, when the advantages of being beautiful don't always translate into greater successes. In fact, being good-looking can cost you opportunities—jobs, assignments, scholarships, promotions, and the like. Not because the halo effect isn't working, but because it's being trumped by something even more powerful: your perceiver's ego lens.

You see, the ego lens, like the trust and power lenses, has a single mission. In this case, it's to see things in such a way that *the perceiver comes out on top.* The ego lens has several strategies that it can deploy to accomplish this mission, each of which I'll describe in detail in this chapter. Put simply, they are as follows:

1. Focus on how the perceiver is better than you or on how the perceiver's group (*us*) is better than your group (*them*).

2. Focus on how you and the perceiver are in the same group (i.e., both of you are *us*) and therefore the perceiver can enjoy your successes and bask in the reflected glory of your awesomeness.

3. Decide that your good qualities are not a threat, because you are not competing with the perceiver for

the same resources or because the perceiver doesn't actually value those particular qualities.

4. If strategies 1, 2, and 3 don't work or aren't applicable, your good qualities and accomplishments are a threat to the perceiver's self-esteem. Therefore, you must be avoided or sabotaged to neutralize the threat.

Let's think about how these strategies might play out for an attractive female candidate applying for a job. If she is being interviewed by another attractive female, then strategy 1 applies—since the interviewer is very attractive herself, it would be relatively easy for her to convince herself that she is a bit *more* attractive than the applicant. These things are subjective, after all. So the threat is eliminated, and the halo effect can work its positive magic.

If the attractive female applicant is instead being interviewed by a male interviewer, then strategy 3 applies. She and her interviewer are not competing for the same resources (e.g., potential lovers), so no threat there, either.

But what if her interviewer is a *less* attractive female? Let's face it—strategy 2 is not going to work. These two people are strangers, and they are potentially competing for the same resources. That they both belong to the group "women" is probably not going to be enough to make the greater attractiveness of one more palatable to the other. For the interviewer, the applicant's attractiveness is a threat. So that leaves strategy 4: avoid or sabotage. And this is exactly what researchers find.

For instance, in one study, attractive applicants for a graduate scholarship received more favorable ratings from opposite-sex raters (halo effect), but not from same-sex raters. Men were unimpressed by a male applicant's handsomeness (no halo effect), and women actually *penalized* female applicants for beauty.[1]

In another study, ratings of attractive job applicants' qualifications depended on the beauty of their beholder. Good-looking raters didn't seem to care one way or another how handsome or beautiful an applicant was, but average-looking raters did—they penalized better-looking same-sex applicants.[2]

Again, raters usually have no idea that they are being influenced by physical attractiveness when making these judgments. The ego lens warps their perception at Phase 1, such that threatening applicants seem genuinely less qualified, less accomplished. No one actually says to himself or herself, much less to others, *I am threatened by this person, so there is no way I'm hiring this applicant.* But that's exactly what happens.

The primary function of the ego lens is to protect and enhance your self-esteem. It wants you to feel good about you. The ego lens works so well, in fact, that almost all of us, other than the clinically depressed, end up with an overall positive view of ourselves and relatively high self-esteem.

Your self-esteem is the sum of all your positive and negative evaluations of yourself—your assessments of your strengths and weaknesses, your memories of your successes and failures. Some of these evaluations are weighted much more heavily than others, because they have to do with things that are more central to your sense of who you are. My evaluations of my abilities as a mother and a psychologist, for example, have a much greater impact on my self-esteem than my (lack of) abilities as an athlete or an artist. Frankly, I don't really care that I have never advanced past stick figures, because being a skilled artist is just not a big part of who I am. But when I drop the ball and forget to pack my daughter's lunch, or when a paper that I've submitted is rejected from a journal, that certainly takes me down a peg.

This is really important to remember: your perceiver's self-esteem is *idiosyncratic*. It's based on what's important to him or her, not what's important to you. If you want to anticipate how a perceiver's ego lens might bias his or her view of you, you're going to need to know a little about what the perceiver cares about. Some assumptions are fairly safe—most people care about their work, their intelligence, their social standing, and their attractiveness. Not all, surely, but a healthy majority. If you pose a threat to your perceiver's self-esteem along any of these dimensions, expect the person's ego lens to kick into gear.

So, how does the perceiver end up with either positive or negative evaluations of his or her own abilities—where is the person's self-esteem coming from? Generally, it comes from a nearly continuous stream of conscious and unconscious comparisons—*how am I doing compared with other people?* And thanks to the ego lens, for most of us, the answer almost always seems to be *better than average*.

Lots of people know this as the Lake Wobegon effect, so named after Garrison Keillor's semi-autobiographical stories, "where all the women are strong, all the men are good-looking, and all the children are above average." Study after study shows that like the residents of Lake Wobegon, the majority of us see ourselves as better than average along just about every meaningful dimension (and a few nonmeaningful ones). Drivers consistently rate themselves as above average in driving skill and safety consciousness. Managers rate themselves as above-average performers and leaders. Business professionals rate themselves as having above-average ethics. College students believe they are healthier, smarter, and more popular than their average peer.

Do me a quick favor, and answer these questions as honestly as you can:

> What do you think the odds are that you will one day find yourself unemployed? Are you more or less likely than other people your own age?

> What do you think the odds are that you will one day make a lot more money than you do now? Are you more or less likely than other people in similar jobs?

Did you say that—compared with others in similar circumstances—you are more likely to get rich and less likely to get canned? Of course you did (unless you are clinically depressed or are trying to outsmart the question). Most of us, thanks to our ego lenses, believe that good things are more likely to happen to us, and bad things less likely to happen to us, than to other people. We believe we are significantly more likely than other people to end up with a career we enjoy, own our own homes, not get divorced, and live past eighty. We think we are less likely to buy a car that turns out to be a lemon, get fired, have a heart attack, develop a drinking problem, or get infected by a venereal disease.[3] *Those things happen to other people, not to me. Especially that last one.*

Psychologists call this *illusory optimism.* And I'll be honest: for the most part, it's a good thing. Believing that things will probably work out will keep us happier and more motivated to keep on keepin' on, even when we are met with challenges and disappointments. Optimism has been linked to greater physical and psychological health, faster recovery from illness, and longer persistence on important life goals. So robust is our need to maintain this overly positive view that the ego lens will work particularly hard to deal with our screwups by subtly changing how we see what happened and who was to blame.

Did you ever notice how quick people are to take credit for their accomplishments and how creatively people seem to deflect blame for their failures? As a college professor, I've heard countless students who performed poorly on one of my tests complain about how the test was unfair or impossible, but never once have I heard from an A student that his or her excellent performance was the result of a test that was too easy. Thanks to the ego lens, it's quite natural to see how our own effort and abilities were the drivers of our successes, while clearly seeing how insurmountable obstacles—particularly those generated by other people—were directly responsible for our failures.

My all-time favorite example of the lengths the ego lens will go comes from an article on auto insurance claims in the *Toronto News* from 1977. Reviewing how people described their own car accidents, the journalist found ample evidence of the ego lens in statements such as these:

> "An invisible car came out of nowhere, struck my car, and vanished."

> "A pedestrian hit me, and went under my car."

> "As I reached an intersection, a hedge sprang up, obscuring my vision."[4]

Man, I really hate it when that happens. Crazy hedges.

Comparing Apples to Other, Lesser Apples

As I mentioned, the essence of self-esteem is comparison. How does the perceiver see himself or herself, in terms of abilities and accomplishments, compared with other people? Psychologist Abraham Tesser argues that a person's self-esteem can be enhanced or threatened by the achievements and shortcomings of another as a function of two factors.[5]

The first is *relevance*. Does the domain of achievement (or failure) really matter to the perceiver? Does it factor into the perceiver's own sense of who he or she is? A professional tennis player is likely to be affected when a rival wins a major tournament, but not when a famous chef opens another successful restaurant. It's not success per se that threatens the player—it's the particular successes that he or she covets.

The second is *closeness*. Is this other successful person a major player in the perceiver's life or an unknown or distant person who can easily be ignored? Perceivers are really only affected—for better or worse—by those whom they see regularly or feel strongly about. This is why sibling rivalry is a thing, and second-cousin-once-removed rivalry isn't. Figure 6-1 shows how it works.

So, if we want to feel good about ourselves—removing the threat to our ego—what should we do? Obviously, who we choose to compare ourselves with will have a tremendous impact on our self-esteem. Which is why, whenever possible, the people we compare ourselves with are chosen very strategically (although unconsciously). To maintain or increase self-esteem,

FIGURE 6-1

How ego threats work

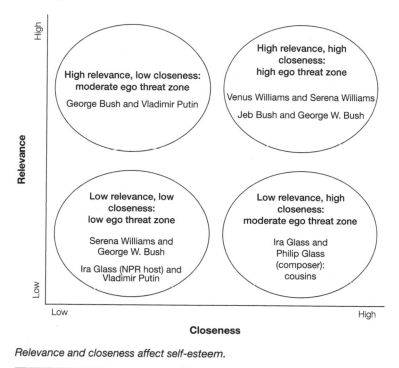

Relevance and closeness affect self-esteem.

we can focus intentionally on close others who are clearly worse off on a relevant dimension—for example, a beloved brother who is so much more scatterbrained than superorganized you. Psychologists call this *downward social comparison.*

As you may have noticed, people do this sort of thing all the time, though they are usually unaware that they are motivated to do it. It's just so easy to find someone who in some way is doing worse than you are. And the net result is feeling really good about yourself. Thank you, ego lens.

Comparing Apples to Really Awesome Apples

What happens when the perceiver can't pick and choose the comparisons—what if the comparison is right there in front of the person, too obvious to ignore? And what if it's not a flattering comparison? In that case, the perceiver will likely feel threatened and, as I mentioned earlier, deal with this threat through one of four ways. If you are the source of the threat, then you may not like the consequences.

Strategy 1: My Apple Is Still Better Than Your Apple

This strategy is the most obvious and straightforward. To reduce the threat created by your abilities or accomplishments, the perceiver can engage in downward comparison along some other dimension—one in which the perceiver is superior to you (or at least thinks he or she is). The perceiver may even exaggerate his or her superiority in this other domain to get the job done. For example, when we're out for a drive and I give my husband grief about speeding, he likes to remind me that I have a long history of driving our car into—and over—curbs. Which is not at all relevant and not even true. Well, OK, it's a little true. But he's exaggerating my proclivity for curb jumping to make himself feel better, because he knows deep down that I am the superior driver. Obviously.

When people use this strategy, you hear a lot of "Yes, but." As in these examples:

Yes, Angela got promoted, but she's a total workaholic; who wants that life?

Yes, Steven is funny, but he's kind of an attention hog.

Yes, Bob's new girlfriend is gorgeous, but she's about as intelligent as an eggplant.

Downward comparison of your group—rather than you individually—is a less obvious but no less effective strategy. The groups to which we belong—our *group identities*—are just as important in determining our sense of who we are as our individual characteristics. (Group identities tend to be based on mutual goals or other commonalities, like race, gender, ethnicity, occupation, family, country, and religion.) Just think of how being a Catholic or a Protestant in Northern Ireland during the last century, a serf or a lord in medieval Europe, or a Hatfield or a McCoy in Kentucky in the 1860s would have shaped every aspect of who you were and how you lived your life. Just think of how being black or white, gay or straight, Christian or Muslim, rich or poor shapes lives in this country, in the here and now: the opportunities and advantages you have, the constraints and pressures you face.

In fact, you could argue—as social psychologists routinely do—that these group identities play a bigger role in determining our self-concept and self-esteem than our individual abilities and accomplishments do. Therefore, it is essential for your self-esteem that you maintain positive views of your own groups and fellow group members, because group members don't merely reflect on you—they are a part of who you are and how you see yourself. They are *us*. So if they aren't smart and brave and good, how can you be? On the other hand, when you are not in the perceiver's group—when you are not *us*—you are *them*. And as decades of research consistently shows, *them* is not such a good thing to be.[6]

What do perceivers think they know about *them*? Well, generally speaking, perceivers know that *they* are all alike, *they* are very different from *us*, and *they* are not as good (smart, hardworking, moral, etc.) as *we* are. *They* are also less trustworthy and less deserving of the resources at our disposal. *Sorority girls are such airheads. IT guys are so nerdy. Millennials are so entitled.* And worse, far worse. Perceivers may never say it out loud—they may never even think it consciously—but their brains are wired to operate under these beliefs implicitly, and that's enough to warp their perception in a big way.

Because perceivers are highly motivated to see their own groups (*us*) as fundamentally better, and because belittling *them* is one way to achieve this goal, researchers consistently find that perceivers engage in more negative stereotyping when they have taken a self-esteem hit. For instance, in one study, researchers asked female participants of Italian descent (who had just been given bogus feedback on an "intelligence test") to evaluate a job candidate according to a résumé and videotaped interview. The experimenters manipulated whether the candidate was perceived as Jewish (Julie Goldberg) or Italian (Maria D'Agastino).

The researchers found that the participants who had previously failed the intelligence test derogated the personality and qualifications of the Jewish candidate (but not the Italian candidate). In prior testing, these participants had demonstrated no particular bias against Jews. In fact, among the participants who received high scores on the intelligence test—and thus had egos that felt more secure—both candidates were rated as equally positive.[7] The *us*-versus-*them* effect only emerged when an ego boost was needed—though in real life, let's face it, that's probably happening a lot.

So, when something about your accomplishments or abilities is threatening to the perceiver, his or her ego lens can try to diminish the threat and restore self-esteem by focusing on how you are one of *them*, and the many dimensions along which *they* are inferior to *us*. As a consequence, you are more likely to find yourself at the receiving end of stereotyping, distrust, and discrimination—all without the perceiver's ever realizing why.

Bottom line: if the perceiver uses the me-versus-you (us-versus-them) strategy to cope with threat, it's not going to be good for you.

Strategy 2: Aren't Our Apples Great? Let's Bask in Reflected Glory!

Another way for perceivers to reduce the threat you pose—a way that will work much more in your favor—is for the perceivers to focus on how you are a part of their group, so the perceivers can share in your triumph as if it were their own. Now, instead of suffering from *them* discrimination, you'll be the beneficiary of *in-group favoritism* and get to take advantage of an array of perception biases that exist to bolster *us* awesomeness.

For starters, perceivers are biased to see other group members as similar to themselves in meaningful and positive ways, and not surprisingly, they like the members more because of it. Perceivers exhibit more fairness, empathy, and compassion toward their own group members. They treat their work more generously and interact more with in-group members than they do with out-group members.

Importantly, being a member of *us* allows the perceiver to not just neutralize the threat your abilities and accomplishments pose, but to enjoy them—to *bask in reflected glory*, or as psychologists call it, to BIRG (rhymes with "surge"). Parents BIRG when their children excel in school or on the playing field, nations BIRG when their athletes take home a gold medal at the Olympics, and African Americans across the United States BIRGed when Barack Obama became the first black president.

We BIRG whenever our fellow group members succeed. Perhaps the most visible example comes from the mania surrounding our favorite sports teams. Did you ever notice how ecstatic fans become when their team wins? They spend hundreds of dollars on "authentic" jerseys and other memorabilia, paint their faces (and sometimes their bodies) with team colors and mascots. The Super Bowl and World Series victories "they" won are routinely remembered as among the greatest moments of these fans' lives, despite the fact that the fans never once set foot on the field.

All this BIRGing can play out in more subtle ways as well. For instance, Robert Cialdini, author of *Influence*, found that among students at the seven universities he observed, the frequency of wearing school sweaters, caps, scarves, and the like was significantly higher on days after the football team won than on days after it lost.[8]

Strategy 3: That's Not My Thing (or, Comparing Apples to Oranges)

Remember that it takes closeness and relevance to create a threat. The achievement and achiever have to matter to the

perceiver. Thus, one strategy the ego lens can use to neutralize threats to self-esteem is to reduce relevance by devaluing
or disengaging from the domain of your success. To do this,
the perceiver basically has to decide that being great at X isn't
important to him or her, personally. It's just not on the person's
agenda.

So your colleague's promotion won't be a threat if you never
wanted the job yourself, and your best friend's getting married
won't get you down if you love being single. In the example
from the beginning of this chapter, being a beautiful female
applicant isn't going to threaten the male interviewer, because
the male interviewer doesn't actually want to be a beautiful
woman. Presumably.

In fact, when a perceiver has a close friend or family member
who achieves something in a domain of low personal relevance,
it's actually a perfect opportunity to BIRG. By associating with
someone whose success is not directly comparable to his own,
the perceiver can actually increase his or her self-esteem.

Siblings and spouses often seem to use this knowledge
strategically—though not necessarily consciously. They
will deliberately focus on developing different domains of
expertise—playing different sports, pursuing different majors,
working in different industries—to make their achievements
less directly comparable and thus avoiding potential self-
esteem threats. I'm sure it's not an accident that my brother
was the jock and I was the bookish one, or that my husband
and his four brothers each chose to pursue a very different
kind of career: health care, law, finance, history, and Silicon
Valley tech. If there had been a sixth brother, he would have
had to have been a chef or possibly a magician.

The most well-known modern example of brothers carving out very different kinds of success would probably be the brothers Emanuel—the Chicago triumvirate whose members have each reached the very top of their respective fields: the mayor of Chicago and former White House chief of staff (Rahm), the prominent medical ethicist and health-care policy adviser (Ezekiel), and Hollywood power player and co-CEO of William Morris Endeavor (Ari). All three brothers are breathtakingly ambitious, famously competitive, and incredibly close—after all these years, still talking to one another almost daily.

But imagine how close they would be today if they had all wanted careers in politics or medicine. If they had all wanted to be the most powerful agent in Hollywood. As Ari once said, "The pressure is that you were judged by the family. Our family never cared about the kid down the block."[9] But if they had all been judged by the same standards—if their achievements had not been apples and oranges, but apples and apples— could the brothers have remained loving allies all these years? The number of families—some you undoubtedly know— torn utterly apart by sibling rivalry would seem to suggest not.

Strategy 4: Avoidance (Apples? What Apples?)

Which brings us to the ego lens's final strategy to reduce threat. If the perceiver can't or won't reduce the relevance of your achievement to his or her own self-esteem, the person can reduce the closeness between the two of you, through *avoidance*. Take the brothers Noel and Liam Gallagher of the multiplatinum band Oasis. The Gallaghers have fought so much over who is more talented and more responsible for their success that they won't even speak to each other anymore. Rivalry among tween darlings the Jonas Brothers put an end to their very lucrative music careers, too. Did you know that even the Everly Brothers could hardly stand one another? Even Serena Williams has said that when she faces off against Venus, she creates a certain amount of mental distance, telling herself, *Right now we're competitors; we can be sisters again later.* I have no idea how often the Manning family—brimming with famous quarterbacks—gets together, but it's got to be tricky for them sometimes, don't you think? Just tossing around a football in the backyard at Dad's house takes on a whole new meaning.

Of course, siblings aren't the only ones who mitigate threat by reducing their closeness. It happens to longtime friends, lovers, and colleagues, too. Looking back at your own life, isn't it all too easy to find examples of relationships that were undermined by your own success or by the other person's? Weren't there times when you felt you needed to hide or downplay the good things happening in your life for the good of your friendship, or when hearing of your friend's streak of good fortune made you want to avoid your friend for a little while?

Reducing closeness in an existing relationship is one way to alleviate ego threat, but it's not without its own kind of pain. Which is why, whenever possible, we try to avoid those relationships that might threaten us from the get-go. For instance, the interviewer I described at the beginning of the chapter might choose not to hire the attractive applicant because of the threat she poses. This decision would successfully reduce closeness—or more accurately, maintain distance—since the two people are unlikely to even see one another again. From a (great) distance, the latter's beauty is no longer threatening.

Dealing with Someone Else's Ego Lens

To deal with the ego lens, first assess the threat you may pose—particularly with someone who doesn't know you well. Ask yourself, *Am I, or could I potentially be, close to the perceiver?* Remember, closeness isn't just about how intimate your relationship is. Closeness is about how much you matter—how much your behavior can affect the perceiver's work and life. So if you are someone the perceiver has to see often or work with directly, or who might be that in the future, you count as close.

Then ask yourself, *Might my abilities or achievements be relevant to the perceiver?* Are you going to have to do or say something that might cast the perceiver's own abilities or achievements in a negative light, like giving him or her a performance review or pointing out an error?

If the answer to these two questions is yes, then you can expect the ego lens and its biases to be hard at work during your interaction. Let us now look at three strategies you can use to mitigate their effects, depending on your circumstances.

Be Modest

Modesty means deliberately doing what you can to be less threatening. I'm not suggesting that you play dumb or in any way try to be someone or something you are not. I am suggesting instead that tooting your own horn with a perceiver who feels threatened is not going to get you the results you are look-ing for. Being humble about your accomplishments and being willing to own up to your past or current difficulties—to be vulnerable and human—can actually be a remarkably effec-tive communication strategy. In so doing, you allow the person you are interacting with to maintain (or even enhance) his or her own self-esteem. At the very least, you put the person at ease, instead of on the defensive.

Be Affirming

Many of the negative effects of ego threat that I've described in this chapter seem to have a simple remedy: affirmation. Remember the college students who failed an intelligence test and then (unknowingly) used stereotypes about Jews to evalu-ate "Julie Goldberg"? In a second version of the study, after receiving the failure feedback, some of the students were given an opportunity to write a paragraph or two about their most important values. (Expressing your own values and why they matter to you is known from prior research to provide a big boost to self-esteem.) Guess what happened? *No* stereotyping. The self-affirming students treated "Julie Goldberg" the same way they treated "Maria D'Agastino"—as an individual, with-out bias. The ego lens had been neutralized.

Fortunately, there are countless ways to affirm another per-son so that he or she feels effective and valuable. (Note: If you think you already are good at sending affirmation signals, you might want to ask someone, because there's a good chance you're not. No offense, but remember the observation from chapter 1: we all communicate much less than we think we do. You say, "Of course my wife knows I think she's beautiful!"

But can your wife remember the last time you told her she looked great?)

Obviously, you can affirm someone by explicitly recognizing or praising the person's words and deeds. You can also affirm through questions—an option that might be a bit more palatable if you aren't very comfortable doling out praise or if you don't know the perceiver particularly well. Ask the person to tell you about his or her current goals, values, proudest moments, dreams for the future. Ask for guidance and perspective on a vexing problem. Anything that allows perceivers to focus, for even a moment, on what is best and most meaningful about themselves and their lives will provide the kind of self-esteem boost necessary to neutralize the ego lens.

Importantly, you need to keep in mind that people don't just want to be seen positively by others—they want to be seen the way they see themselves. Psychologists call this the desire for *self-verification*, and it is a profound and universal need. People become really uncomfortable when they get compliments (or criticism) they feel they genuinely don't deserve. What this means for you is that praising someone for a quality they don't believe they possess can backfire on you big-time. The best way to steer clear of this problem is to stick with truthful affirmations. In other words, affirm the abilities and accomplishments that you have direct evidence of—the ones that you know to be authentic and genuinely admire.

Be Us, *Not* Them

The ego lens isn't all bad. There are great benefits to be had, for instance, when your perceiver chooses to BIRG over your accomplishments. But how can you encourage him or her to see you as a part of Team Us, rather than Team Them?

The surprising answer is, it doesn't take much. Research suggests that what counts as a group you both belong to—and therefore what it takes to bring about the powerful in-group/out-group effects that I have described—can be trivial. For instance, in the laboratory, strong in-group favoritism is produced when people are placed into blue-eyed versus brown-eyed groups or categorized according to the color of the shirt they happen to be wearing. In one study, participants were asked to rate their liking for abstract paintings and were randomly told that they preferred the paintings by either "Kandinsky" or "Klee." In another, they were asked to estimate the number of jelly beans in a jar and were told (again, randomly) that they were either "overestimators" or "underestimators." Subsequently, the researchers found that "Kandinsky fans" much preferred one another to "Klee fans" and that "overestimators" believed that their personalities were more similar to one another than to "underestimators."[10]

As Henri Tajfel, one of the early giants of research on social identity, discovered, us-versus-them thinking happens even when you assign groups on the basis of a coin toss—*and even when people know it was based on a coin toss*. In his coin-toss studies, Tajfel witnessed in-group favoritism, dislike of the out-group, and the perception that the out-group was meaningfully different, even when objectively it could not possibly be.[11]

So given that it doesn't take much to make a group, all you are looking for to emphasize your *us*-ness is any sort of commonality. Obviously, the more meaningful and salient your commonalities, the more effective they will be—but even something as simple as pointing out that you both are big fans of Bruce Springsteen can be enough to move you from a *them* to an *us*.

Before your next encounter with a perceiver who you suspect sees you as a *them*, take a moment to search your memory for some experiences or attributes you might share. These need to be true, by the way—making something up will probably create more problems for you than it will solve. Work some references to these commonalities into your conversation as naturally as you can, in whatever ways you are comfortable with, and then watch how powerfully and positively the dynamic between you and the perceiver shifts, as your perceiver's ego lens recognizes that you are not a liability, but an asset in the ego lens's never-ending quest to end up on top.

Key Takeaways

- The ego lens has one goal—to protect (and enhance) the perceiver's self-esteem. Thanks to its robust functioning, most of us tend to see ourselves as smarter, more attractive, and more morally upstanding than the average person. We take credit for our successes and blame our failures on the circumstances, other people, or dumb luck. All of this isn't exactly admirable, but it gets the job done.

- The extent that a perceiver's self-esteem can be threatened by your accomplishments and abilities is a function of how *relevant* they are (i.e., does the perceiver want the same accomplishments and abilities?) and how *close* you are (i.e., are you an active part of his or her life?). When relevance or closeness is low, the threat is diminished and you will be seen more accurately.

- When both relevance and closeness are high, you are in trouble—the perceiver will somehow have to diminish you (mentally) or maintain greater distance from you to protect his or her self-esteem.

- These ego lens processes go beyond individuals to the groups to which we belong. A success for someone in my group is *my* success, while a success for someone in your group is a threat to mine.

- This is why forming a sense of *us* with your perceiver is so important—when you are part of the same group that your perceiver belongs to, your accomplishments and abilities can be a source of self-esteem for him or her, too.

- Two other techniques—*modesty* and *affirmation*—can be useful in stopping an ego threat before it starts.

Part III

Lenses for Particular Personalities

Chapter 7

Eager Reward-Seekers and Vigilant Risk-Mitigators

Imagine what it must be like to be Sir Richard Branson. I'm not talking about what it's like to be a multibillionaire or befriend Nelson Mandela—although those both sound pretty good. Imagine what it must be like to *think* like Branson. The billionaire philanthropist and serial entrepreneur has led a life jam-packed with risk and adventure. (As I write this, he is probably bungee jumping off something, somewhere.) I like to think that over the course of his life, his inner monologue has sounded something like this:

> "Should I start a chain of record stores? Yes. Great idea!"

> "Why not a record label? Why not, indeed?"

> "And then, I don't know, maybe an airline? What about trains? Perhaps a mobile company? My own line of soda? Vodka? Alternative fuels? Circumvent the globe

in a hot air balloon? Wait . . . what about space tourism? Yes, yes, yes, yes, yes, yes, *yes!*"

. . .

The trust, power, and ego lenses are worn by all of us, at one time or another. But there are other lenses that alter perception—some that are specific to particular types of people, whose personalities predispose them to see others with unique biases. Let's look at some of these personality-driven lenses.

In general, what do you spend more time thinking about: how you can end up better off, or how you can hang on to what you've already got? Yes, I know this probably seems like an odd question, because both goals are obviously important. Each of us engages in activities whose purpose is both to enhance our lives and to protect what we already hold dear. We launch new businesses, take courses to develop our skills, scan online dating sites for potential partners, get face-lifts, plan vacations, and buy lottery tickets—all to get to a place that's better than we are now. We also save for retirement, pay our mortgages, get our kids vaccinated, load antivirus software onto our computers, and get that weird-looking mole checked out—all to stay safe and secure and to maintain the quality of life we've come to know.

But while all of us, ideally, would like to end up better off *and* hang on to what we already have, most of us put more emphasis on one or the other. In other words, some of us tend to see what we do—the goals we pursue at work and at home—as being first and foremost about advancing, while the rest of us see what we do as being mostly about staying safe.

This difference in how we see the world and what we want out of it creates two distinct lenses: what psychologists call *promotion focus* and *prevention focus*.

A promotion-focused perceiver sees opportunities for achievement, reward, and accomplishment all around. In the language of economics, life becomes about *maximizing gains* and *avoiding missed opportunities*. Richard Branson is a promotion-focused person to a T. A prevention-focused perceiver, on the other hand, sees dangers that must be avoided and responsibilities that must be fulfilled. In economic terms, life is about *minimizing losses* and *maintaining the status quo*.[1]

For the record, there is no right or wrong way to look at the world. One of these lenses is not, generally speaking, better than the other one. We now know, from decades of research, that promotion- and prevention-focused people can be equally effective, lead equally successful lives, and be equally satisfied with them. But people will work very differently to reach the goals they pursue. They will use different kinds of strategies, have different strengths and preferences, and be prone to different kinds of mistakes. Looking through one lens, they will be motivated by applause; looking through the other, by criticism. One lens may lead them to give up too soon; the other lens may keep them from knowing when to quit.

The promotion and prevention lenses will also bias perceivers to find different kinds of arguments and evidence persuasive. As a result, subtle changes in language can have a profound effect on your ability to really get through to them. So if you want to communicate successfully with your colleagues, your boss—even your spouse or children—you're going to need to understand which of these two lenses they are looking through.

The Promotion Lens: Nothing Ventured, Nothing Gained

Even if you yourself rarely look through the promotion lens, you will immediately recognize the people who do. Promotion-focused people are the risk takers, the rule breakers, the adventurers. It's the guy you went to college with whose crazy idea for a start-up made him a multimillionaire. (It's also the guy you went to college with whose start-up went bust, because his idea really was crazy, and now he lives in his parents' basement.)

Just like that most famous rule of improvisational acting, to every opportunity that knocks, promotion-focused people answer, "Yes! And . . ." Here a gain, there a gain, everywhere nothing but potential gains, rewards, and advancements. (Also, lots and lots of ways to fail spectacularly. But the promotion lens tends to obscure that part of the picture.)

You see, when people wear the promotion lens, they are naturally more open-minded, less cautious, more willing to consider many possibilities, and quicker to generate them. Promotion-focused people feel free to be more exploratory and abstract in their thinking. The solutions they come up with are more creative and more innovative. People using the promotion lens are also particularly good at picking up on connecting themes, synthesizing information, and identifying opportunities when they present themselves.

When promotion-focused people are really motivated, it looks and feels like eagerness—they can't wait to go for it. They work quickly, rushing to see their ideas come to fruition and wanting to be ready when the next opportunity comes along. They are usually optimists, in large part because they need to be. Promotion motivation is at its highest when the outlook is bright. So obstacles get downplayed, challenges get underestimated, and past failures are all too quickly forgotten.

It won't surprise you, then, that the same confidence that fuels promotion motivation comes at a cost. Looking through the promotion lens, the perceivers will rarely see the need to consider what will happen if things go wrong or to create a plan B. They'll be unprepared for bumps in the road. They'll give little thought to maintaining the gains they have already accumulated or protecting the progress already made. Promotion-focused people will get in over their heads, saying yes to too many things at once. Even someone as successful as Richard Branson has a few rather spectacular failures to his name. (Have you ever had Virgin Vodka? No? I thought not.)

If you have—or have ever had—a boss who sees through a promotion lens, then you know all too well how that can be both a blessing and a curse. The enthusiasm of promotion-focused people can be infectious, and their generally positive, open-minded outlook can help foster an environment where new ideas and fresh approaches are welcome. They are rarely micromanagers, so if you have an independent spirit, it can flourish under a promotion-focused leader. On the other hand, you will probably receive far less guidance and feedback than you would like, your mistakes will go unchecked, important details will go unnoticed, and you may find yourself crushed under the mountain of work that your boss will assign you, as he or she eagerly says yes to every potential project that comes into your group's orbit.

Perhaps it would be better to work under someone who runs a tighter ship? Well, let's see . . .

The Prevention Lens: Measure Twice, Cut Once

Looking through the prevention lens and seeing a world filled with dangers to be avoided like potholes on a highway, people naturally acquire a very different set of skills and preferences. The prevention-focused are thorough, deliberate, and reliable. These are the people who balance their checkbooks monthly, never run out of clean underwear, and can get you a copy of any important document they've been given in the last ten years in three minutes or less, because they know exactly where it is.

Looked at through the prevention lens, abstraction and creativity seem reckless and time-consuming. Prevention-focused thinking is concrete and specific and heavy on the details. It leads to better memory not only for what has already happened, but also for what still needs to be done. It's also time-consuming—sometimes painfully so. Give an assignment to a prevention-minded person, and don't hold your breath waiting for him or her to finish it. They hate mistakes, and the only way to avoid errors entirely is to take it slow. (Legal departments are filled with prevention-focused people, by the way. Which explains a lot.)

When you are obsessed with avoiding mistakes, it's only natural for you to become concerned that the people who report to you might be making them, too. Prevention-focused leaders have a tendency to tightly supervise—even micromanage— their employees and to have trouble delegating important tasks to the control of others. On the other hand, they are more likely to provide necessary guidance and feedback and to have a more realistic sense of what you can accomplish with the time and resources at your disposal.

Admittedly, prevention-focused people aren't the most innovative people in the word—but they do have a distinct advantage when it comes to analytical thinking and reasoning. Studies show that while looking through the promotion lens leads to greater creativity, the people who look through the prevention lens are the ones who can tell a high-quality, usable, creative idea from one that will never cut the mustard.

Prevention-minded people are also cautious. They tend to say no to opportunities more often, having what psychologists call a more *conservative bias*. They are reluctant to disengage from one activity to try another or to change the status quo, always preferring the devil they know to the one they don't. But their conservative nature also makes them less likely than their risk-loving promotion lens colleagues to procrastinate, for fear that they won't have time to get the job done.

The prevention-focused expect to encounter obstacles, so they spend a lot of time thinking about how to deal with them. They don't just have a plan B; they have a plan C, D, and possibly E. They take nothing for granted and are prepared for the worst. Again, this doesn't necessarily make them fun at parties—but it makes them invaluable members of the team when things do go wrong.

And while it is really easy to come up with a long list of well-known promotion-focused people, when I try to think of a famous prevention-focused person, I have a really hard time coming up with even one. That's because the people who look through the prevention lens are always the unsung heroes of any success story. They don't rush in to rescue people from disasters—they are the ones who make sure disasters don't happen in the first place. They're making sure that the airplane you are flying in doesn't lose an engine midair, that the medicine you are taking won't accidentally kill you, and that there's a plan in place if your city is struck by a hurricane, a tornado, or a bout of swine flu. Keeping things running smoothly won't make you famous. So if you are prevention focused, you probably deserve a lot more thanks than you are likely to ever get.

Looked at through the prevention lens, motivation feels like vigilance, rather than eagerness. The thing about vigilance is that—unlike eagerness—it actually increases in response to negative feedback or self-doubt. Think about this observation for a minute, because it will probably blow your mind a little. For the prevention-minded, believing you might fail is really motivating. There's nothing like the looming possibility of failure to get your prevention juices flowing. Too much confidence or effusive praise—the kind of stuff the promotion-minded can't get enough of—will lead a prevention-minded person to let down his or her guard and actually undermine the person's motivation.

To be clear, it's not that the prevention lens leads you to believe that you *will* fail. True pessimism is never good for anyone. Instead, it leads you to believe that you *might* fail, if you don't do everything in your power to keep that from happening. Failure is possible, so you need to be on your guard. Psychologists call this quality *defensive pessimism*, and it is as strong a predictor of success in the classroom and the workplace as optimism—whether or not it works for you depends on the lens you are looking through.[2]

So, you know that colleague you have who always seems to be doubting himself or herself, even after enjoying a long string of successes? The one who looks physically uncomfortable when singled out for praise? The one you keep telling to lighten up? You should probably leave colleagues like this alone. They know what they're doing. (And if *you* are that person, then by all means continue to tune out the cheerleaders for positivity. They mean well, but they just aren't looking through your lens.)

Identifying Someone's Promotion or Prevention Lens

In addition to the different behavioral tendencies I've already mentioned, like the preference for speed versus accuracy, or risk taking versus risk avoidance, there are a few other cues you can use to identify your own lens and your perceiver's. Let's explore these cues now.

Age

Research suggests that promotion focus is most common among the young, because young people are particularly preoccupied with the future—with living their dreams.[3] In your teens and twenties, you don't have many responsibilities, and you are constantly being told that you can achieve anything you set your mind to. You look and feel great. This is more or less a recipe for strong promotion focus.

As we get older, signs of mortality begin to appear. Before we know it, there are bills to be paid, a job we can't afford to lose, a home to care for, and children to raise. The older we get, the more we want to hang on to what we've already got—the things that mean the most to us, that we've worked so hard to obtain. We also have more experience with pain and loss, so we think more and more about how to avoid them. We find ourselves increasingly looking through the prevention lens.

Emotional Tone

Picture one of your colleagues—anyone you know reasonably well. Now, try to recall a time that this colleague received good news—a time when he or she was happy. Maybe a project came in under budget or was completed on time. Maybe a customer was particularly pleased with your colleague's work. What did "happy" look like? Was it the high-energy, joyful kind of happy? Were there lots of big smiles and some well-deserved patting of his or her own back? *Yeah, I knew they were going to be happy with it. They love me. Wait until they see what I do for them on the next project!*

Or, was it a low-energy, calm kind of happy? Did you see your colleague's shoulders relax, a quick flash of a smile, and a long exhale? Did it feel a bit more like relief than joy? *Well, that could have gone a lot worse.*

Promotion- and prevention-minded people differ very reliably in the way they emotionally experience successes and failures. Looking through the promotion lens, where life is all about potential advancement and gain, success makes you feel ecstatic, elated—or more informally, really psyched. When things don't work out as planned—when you fail to advance, or miss out on the reward—you feel sad, dejected, and, in more severe cases, depressed. Life through the prevention lens, on the other hand, is all about avoiding danger and loss—so moments of success are cause for relaxation, for calm and peace. *Danger avoided! Phew!* When danger is still lurking, however, you are likely to feel tense, anxious, and—when the threat seems particularly dire—downright terrified.[4]

Job Role

When you look through a promotion lens (or a prevention lens), some kinds of work—and therefore particular types of organizational roles—are just a much better fit for you. A role that fits your motivational focus will allow you to capitalize on your strengths while simultaneously minimizing the impact of your weaknesses. It's not surprising, then, that organizational psychologists find more promotion-focused people in the "creative and artistic" occupations—like musician, copywriter, and consultant. This kind of work rewards innovation, risk taking, and outside-the-box thinking. Prevention-focused people, on the other hand, are often to be found in "conventional and realistic" occupations—like accountant, engineer, and contract lawyer—where diligence, thoroughness, and accuracy are highly valued.[5] And when people are working together on a team, a person's dominant lens may end up determining the role he or she plays—for instance, among semiprofessional soccer players in Germany, researchers found greater promotion focus among the strikers (the offensive players) and greater prevention focus among defenders and goalies.[6]

Table 7-1 summarizes the typical thinking styles, outlooks, and other key characteristics of promotion-focused and prevention-focused people.

TABLE 7-1

Is your perceiver looking through the promotion or prevention lens?

	Promotion lens	Prevention lens
Thinking style	Abstract Open-minded Holistic	Concrete Thorough Detail-oriented
Working style	Speedy Prone to error	Slow Accurate
Outlook	Optimistic Comfortable with risk	Defensively pessimistic Risk averse
Strengths	Creativity Innovation Identifying opportunities	Analysis and evaluation Preparedness Reliability
Emotional tone	Cheerful to depressed	Calm to anxious
Occupations	Artist Consultant Inventor	Administrator Accountant Engineer

How to Speak Your Perceiver's Motivational Language

A good friend of mine, "Tom," recently brought to his boss's attention a product that would allow the company to take its social media efforts to a whole new level and might significantly improve its image. The product would be an industry first and not entirely without risk, but with huge potential payoff.

After hearing his pitch, his boss asked, "Are any of our competitors using this?"

"No," Tom replied, feeling that this was a strong selling point—a competitive edge.

"Well," his boss responded, "then I don't think we want to stick our necks out and be the first, do we?"

Huh?

Tom was disappointed, but not at all surprised. For every promotion lens manager out there trying to encourage innovation, there seem to be ten prevention lens managers standing squarely in the way of it. I spend a lot of time talking to people about motivation and growth, and everywhere I go, I hear complaints like these:

> "I just can't get my boss to take the risk."

> "There's a huge opportunity here, and we're missing it."

> "We just follow trends; we don't ever create them."

It's incredibly frustrating to know you have a real winner of an idea on your hands, something that could really shake things up, and not be able to get it past your boss's prevention-minded biases. Not that the cautious, conservative approach doesn't have its advantages—but ultimately an organization cannot grow without embracing *some* risk.

So, how can you get your cautious boss, who is weighed down with responsibilities and understandably antirisk, to go out on a limb and embrace a great, albeit risky, idea? The key is to stop fighting his or her prevention lens and to work with it instead.

In the end, it's all about language. You may be thinking of your great idea as an opportunity for gain, but you can always reframe it as *an opportunity for avoiding loss*. To persuade a prevention-minded person, you want to emphasize how the course of action you are advocating can keep your company safe and secure—how it will help your company avoid making a terrible mistake.

For instance, you may be thinking of a new social media venture as a chance to get in front of the pack, but your boss might be more persuaded if you phrased it as a way to *not fall behind*. ("Everyone is moving in this direction. It's inevitable. We could lose market share if we aren't prepared for the future.")

In general, it's important to frame your communications in a way that is persuasive to the kind of person you're talking to. Figure out if the decision maker is looking through the promotion or prevention lens, and pitch accordingly. Remember that even the most timid, prevention-minded person will gladly take a risk, once you help him or her understand why it would be a greater risk *not* to.

Promotion-minded people generally respond well to arguments framed in terms of potential gains, possible benefits, and the good things that will happen if they agree to do X (whether X is to approve a project, compromise on a contentious issue, accept change, or provide more support to a colleague). The prevention-minded are more persuaded by what they might lose, mistakes that can be avoided, and the bad things that will happen if they *don't* agree to do X. The promotion lens is looking for why the perceiver should say yes, while the prevention lens is searching for reasons to not say no.

These differences in framing can translate into big differences in motivation and performance. For instance, in one of my favorite studies, players in a regional league of the German

Football Association were told that they would be practic-
ing penalty shot kicking. (FYI, playing in a regional league
in Germany is a very big deal. These players are incredible
athletes.)

Before taking the first penalty kick, the coach approached
each player individually and framed the task in one of the following ways:

> "You are going to shoot five penalties. Your *aspiration* is
> to *score* at least three times."

> "You are going to shoot five penalties. Your *obligation* is
> to *not miss* more than two times."

Either way, the goal was to score three or more times out of
five—so you wouldn't really expect a little difference in word-
ing to change performance for players like these, who were all
highly practiced in kicking penalty shots and highly motivated
to perform at their best. But motivationally, there was a big
difference—the kind of difference that can mean winning or
losing the game. Promotion players performed significantly better when told to "score three times out of five." The effect was
even larger for prevention-minded players, who scored nearly
twice as often when told to "not miss more than two times."[7]

In addition to responding to positive framing, promotion
people prefer more-abstract thinking and rely on feelings and
intuition to make decisions. They are more strongly influenced
by *inspirational role models*—people who did things the right
way and enjoyed great success because if it.

The prevention-minded don't give a damn about your feelings and intuition—they, like *Star Trek*'s Spock, want details,

reasons, and evidence before they'll go along with your plan. And if you want to influence them, spare them the inspirational role model and hit them with a discomfort-inducing cautionary tale about the people who did everything wrong and suffered the consequences.

By now you may be wondering if promotion and prevention people can actually get along with each other at all, since the opportunities for conflict seem endless. Fortunately, research suggests that the best partnerships (and by "best," I mean something like "most adaptive and mutually satisfying") may in fact be the Odd Couples.[8] For example, among dating and married romantic partners, those with different lenses enjoyed greater relationship satisfaction than all-promotion or all-prevention pairings. The researchers found that the benefit of this mixed pairing stemmed from the clear advantages of being able to divide and conquer various activities.

After all, couples—like other teams—usually have goals related to both advancement and security. They need to help each other both to innovate and to fulfill their responsibilities. So each person can take on the tasks that he or she is best suited for, knowing that the partner has got the rest covered. Within mixed-lens teams, there is the potential to be more balanced—to be optimistic *and* realistic—because the partnership contains both the promotion and the prevention points of view.

To capitalize on the strengths of both lenses on a team, rather than getting bogged down in conflicts over whose approach is the best one, you need two things: respect for the advantages that both promotion and prevention thinking can yield (without valuing one over the other) and strategic use of the motivational language that your team member will be most responsive to.

Use the right kind of language when you make requests or proposals to your colleagues (and your family and friends)—language that is tailored to their own way of seeing the world—and you will be astounded by the difference in your ability to communicate and influence effectively. Research shows that fitting your approach to the promotion and prevention lenses makes you significantly more believable and trustworthy, makes your ideas more convincing, and gives them greater value in the eyes of your perceiver.[9] Communication that doesn't fit, on the other hand, can sabotage the very best ideas and intentions without either you or your perceiver ever realizing why.

Key Takeaways

- When people are promotion focused, they are trying to end up better off than they are now. They embrace risk, work quickly, seize opportunities, and generate more creative and innovative ideas. They are also more likely to make mistakes, fail to foresee problems, and be overly optimistic.

- When people are prevention focused, they are trying to hang on to what they already have and to keep things running smoothly. They are cautious, deliberate, and analytical. They plan effectively and are always prepared. They are also overly risk averse, inflexible, and too wedded to the status quo.

- Everyone uses both focuses, depending on the context. But people also tend to have a dominant focus—a promotion or prevention lens that they are generally looking through.

- Speaking the right motivational language when communicating with your perceiver is key. For a promotion-focused perceiver, frame your ideas in terms of potential gains or wins—as ways of ending up better off than you are now. Be optimistic, and appeal to emotion. For a prevention-focused perceiver, frame your ideas in terms of avoiding losses or mistakes—as ways of staying safe and secure. Be a realist, and enlist cold, hard facts.

Chapter 8

The Clingy, Anxious Perceiver and the Aloof, Avoidant Perceiver

I have two dear friends who are sisters. They are both highly educated, brilliant businesswomen who have enjoyed quite a bit of career success. But knowing them as well as I do, I believe that they would have enjoyed a great deal more success by now if they were both just a little bit better at dealing with people.

They have very different problems when it comes to their (lack of) social skills. One sister, whom I'll call "Sarah," is needy, overly accommodating, and highly sensitive to rejection, while "Emily" is aloof and has difficulty making connections with others. But both of these problems stem in large part from their childhood and are manifestations of a single (and all too common) influence: neglectful parents.

It's not that Sarah and Emily didn't have enough food to eat or clothes to wear. And they weren't beaten or yelled at, or even punished particularly often. Their parents—like many others—were just very preoccupied with their own lives. The parents married and had children very young—in fact, you could argue they were still practically children themselves, who still quite naturally wanted to do all the selfish things that young people generally want to do. They wanted to go to parties and socialize with their friends. They wanted to go on trips and have adventures. And they wanted to build successful careers—following their own dreams. Their two little girls seemed to mostly get in the way. Or at least, looking back, that's how it seems to Sarah and Emily.

Roughly half of the adults in the United States have difficulty relating to other people in adaptive, healthy ways, because their mental models of what relationships are like are still based on the maladaptive relationships of their childhood. It is in childhood that we learn that people can—or can't—be trusted to be there for us, and we carry those lessons with us into our homes and workplaces as adults.

. . .

Psychologist John Bowlby, one of the most influential figures in the study of child development, identified three ways in which infants become attached to their caregivers.[1] *Securely attached* children have caregivers who are responsive to their needs—the adults can be counted on to provide comfort and to be helpful and understanding. These children seek out their caregivers for support when sad or frightened, but otherwise feel safe to venture out and explore the world. They are the kids who will happily play with other children on the playground until they fall and scrape their knees. Then they run crying to Mommy or Daddy (or Nanny), get kissed and hugged and bandaged up, and run happily back to their friends for more play.

Being responsive isn't the same thing as indulging the child's every whim or giving the child everything he or she asks for. Being responsive means showing concern and affection and making the child feel safe and well-cared-for. Above all, it means consistently doing these things.

When a child feels that his or her caregiver's responses are loving but *not* reliable—the caregiver is sometimes there for the child, but often isn't—or when love feels contingent on the child's doing everything exactly right, then he or she will most likely develop *anxious attachment*. Anxiously attached children (which make up about 30 percent of all children in the United States) are needy and clingy. They are deeply worried that their caregiver might not be there for them when he or she is needed, so they act out to get the caregiver's attention. And they are easily upset when that attention isn't given. These are the children who cry and scream all morning about going to the playground, only to get there and throw a tantrum and refuse to play with the other children or leave their caregiver's side.

My friend Sarah was one of those children. According to her sister, she would cling to her parents whenever they were around, until they would inevitably get annoyed and force her to let go. She would make big scenes and ruin family gatherings, just so her parents would fully focus on her. She never ventured far from home—in fact, she lives only a few blocks from her parents' house and stops by nearly every day. Often, Sarah will use those visits to complain to her parents about how they "ruined" her life, how she would have turned out differently if they had just given a damn about her. Then she'll turn around and buy them an expensive gift or send them on a vacation—anything and everything to get the validation from them she desperately craves.

When caregivers are perceived as reliably *un*responsive, on the other hand—when they generally just can't be bothered to provide loving support to the child—then he or she will probably develop *avoidant attachment.* Avoidant children (about 20 percent of children in the United States) want very little to do with their caretakers. They don't worry about not getting the affection and attention they desire, because they *expect* not to. These children neither cry over going to the park nor even ask about it very often, because they assume the caregiver won't take them, so they'd better just amuse themselves. Sarah's sister Emily was this sort of child. According to Sarah, it was as if Emily just checked out of the family around the time she was five and never checked back in. She kept to herself, kept her own counsel, and never complained about the attention she never received. When it was time to go to college, Emily didn't apply to a single school within a thousand miles of home, and she hasn't lived within a thousand miles of home since.

Both anxious and avoidant attachment are the product of neglect—though, as I said earlier, not necessarily the kind of neglect that gets your children taken from you by Social Services. These kids may have a totally normal-looking life— food to eat, clothes to wear, toys to play with, and a nice roof over their heads. It's the attention and emotional support they aren't getting enough of. Perhaps their caregivers are preoccupied with other things, or perhaps the caregivers themselves were the products of this same sort of neglect and don't know how to give support that they never received themselves.

Whatever the reason, these early experiences of responsiveness and neglect shape the child's view of what relationships are, what can be expected of him or her, and whether other people can be trusted. Decades of research on attachment has found that these views are fairly stable once they are established and that we see even our adult relationships—with romantic partners, friends, and colleagues—through the lenses that these models create.[2] Psychologists sometimes identify attachment style in adults by asking them to read descriptions of each style (secure, anxious, avoidant) and seeing which description fits them best.

The Secure Lens

A securely attached adult would describe himself or herself like this: "I find it relatively easy to get close to others and am comfortable depending on them and having them depend on me. I don't often worry about being abandoned or about someone getting too close to me."[3]

Roughly 50 percent of adults say that this description fits them best.[4] I'm not going to describe this lens in depth, because if your perceiver is looking through it, frankly it's just not going to cause problems for you. People looking through the secure lens are relatively easy to get along with and don't have trust issues. It's the other two lenses you need to worry about.

The Anxious Lens

Here is how adults with anxious attachment might describe themselves: "I find that others are reluctant to get as close as I would like. I often worry that my partner doesn't really love me or won't want to stay with me. I want to merge completely with another person, and this desire sometimes scares people away."[5]

Does that sound like anyone you know (or possibly someone you dated)? I'll bet it does.

The anxiously attached have felt the pain of abandonment before, and they know all too well that it might happen again. So they are constantly seeking closeness, while simultaneously constantly worrying that the people they want to be close to don't return the feeling. They doubt their own self-worth, question whether they are even lovable, and look to others for validation. It's not exactly that they have low self-esteem—it's more accurate to say that their self-esteem fluctuates wildly, depending on how much validation they are getting.

When they become tense or fearful, they get clingy, jealous, highly emotional, and really, really needy. (Ironically, these are the very behaviors that tend to drive people away.) The anxiously attached can also be caring and giving, but there's something off about the way they care—it's impulsive, controlling, and sometimes overwhelming. It feels almost as if it's more about them than it is about you. And it *is* about them, which is why it feels that way. They are too wrapped up in their own concerns and fears to engage in the kind of perspective taking necessary to give high-quality support.

One of the most troublesome aspects of the anxiously attached is their tendency to see injuries and slights where there are none and to make a big deal out of interpersonal problems that really shouldn't be such a big deal. Columbia psychologist Geraldine Downey coined the term *rejection sensitivity* to describe this three-part phenomenon: the perceiver (1) expects to be rejected, (2) is quick to perceive rejection in ambiguous circumstances, and then (3) overreacts to rejection (real or imagined).[6] The perceiver's lens is skewed in such a way that the smallest things—an e-mail not returned, an appointment you are late for, a compliment not given—feel like a deliberate slap in the face or a sign of your true feelings for the person.

People with strong rejection sensitivity, like my friend Sarah, tend to be over-accommodating and ingratiating to win favor. When people meet Sarah for the first time, they find her warm, funny, and generally charming. It's what happens later—the neediness, the emotionality, the hurt and hostility—that ultimately ruins everything. Sarah has changed jobs every year or two, and always because of interpersonal conflicts with her supervisor or colleagues. ("He was out to get me." "She deliberately undermined me at every step." "They all kept me out of the loop.") She's also been engaged three times, but had each engagement broken off by a fiancé who wondered if he could handle life with a woman so prone to bouts of jealousy *and* suffocating levels of affection.

The great irony of all this is that, in principle, rejection sensitivity develops in the service of trying to prevent rejection. The anxious lens causes these people to see rejection everywhere because they are scared to death of it, and they are trying to keep it from happening again. But the consequences of rejection sensitivity are so interpersonally unpleasant that the strategy generally backfires, producing the very rejection they sought to avoid.[7]

The Avoidant Lens

Here's a typical self-description of avoidant attachment in adults: "I am somewhat uncomfortable being close to others; I find it difficult to trust them completely, difficult to allow myself to depend on them. I am nervous when anyone gets too close, and often, love partners want me to be more intimate than I feel comfortable being."[8]

As a result of their early experiences, like those of my friend Emily, people with this attachment style have learned that other people fundamentally cannot be trusted to be responsive to their needs. So they've decided to go it alone—they have become an island unto themselves. In fact, they often take pride in their self-sufficiency and independence and are likely to think relatively highly of themselves and relatively less of everyone else for being so pathetically needy.

People who look through the avoidant lens prefer to maintain emotional distance, even in their closer relationships. And they don't disclose things about themselves readily, because too much intimacy makes them feel vulnerable. I have an avoidant male friend who told me that despite having been in back-to-back lengthy monogamous relationships for about fifteen years, he hadn't told a woman that he loved her in that entire time. He just felt that this was a line he dared not cross—that some sort of nightmare of intimacy and mutual interdependence would unfold if he did. I do not envy the women he dated.

Incidentally, think twice before you offer emotional support to avoidant people, because they generally don't want your support, and they would really prefer that you not count on theirs.

In part, this reluctance is because they often don't know how to give support, having not received much of it themselves. It's also because they have very little use for reciprocity—they don't feel they can count on it. If they do show support of some kind, it tends to be motivated by a sense of obligation rather than genuine desire, which ultimately undermines the relationship further.

. . .

Table 8-1 illustrates the key differences between perceivers who use an anxious lens and those who use an avoidant one. Consult it whenever you've got an interpersonally difficult colleague on your hands, to help you figure out exactly what you are dealing with.

TABLE 8-1

Are your perceivers looking through the anxious or avoidant lens?

	Anxious lens	Avoidant lens
Emotional tone	Worrying Needy Quick to anger	Chilly Disinterested Difficult to anger
What they want	Constant validation Evidence of affection and loyalty	To keep you at a distance To not depend on you, and to not be depended on
How their relationships end	From self-sabotaging oversensitivity to rejection	From self-sabotaging unwillingness to open up
What they hate most	Broken promises Ambiguity Loneliness	Obligation Forced intimacy Vulnerability

Speaking Your Perceiver's Attachment Language

Psychologists don't know as much about anxious and avoidant attachment in adults as they do about promotion focus and prevention focus. That's because most of the research done on attachment focuses on infants and little kids. However, there are still a few research-based strategies you can use to communicate more clearly with someone perceiving you through one of these lenses.

If you suspect that your perceiver is looking through the anxious lens, you should start by taking a deep breath, because this is going to require some effort and patience. You are dealing, fundamentally, with a frightened person—someone who is not above hurting you first just to keep you from hurting him or her. It's not going to be easy. Here are some key approaches to rely on:

- **Practice empathy.** When a person with an anxious lens gets defensive or lashes out, ask yourself, *Why does he or she feel threatened right now?* Try to look at things through the anxious lens—what could be the perceived rejection? Doing this will not only help you to understand the problem, but will create feelings of empathy that will guide you in the direction of a solution.

- **Don't take it personally.** Again, this is really not about you—it's about what happened to the perceiver a long time ago. If you can keep calm and remain engaged, it will help him or her to do so.

- **Avoid ambiguity.** The truth is, a lot of ambiguity would be cleared up completely if we took a little extra trouble to make ourselves clear. Your perceiver is less likely to read your words and actions as rejecting if you take pains to project your true intentions.

- **Be reliable.** It's never a good idea to blow people off or not keep your word, but it is a particularly bad idea when you are dealing with someone looking through the anxious lens.

Consider a hypothetical. You have added a new member, Julia, to your team, and you are eager to involve her in the team's current projects. So you ask her to take the lead on an upcoming conference—a role that would usually be played by your anxiously attached employee, David. Now that you know about the anxious lens, what should you do?

By taking a moment to see it all from David's perspective, you realize immediately that this situation that will create ambiguity for David. *Why did you assign Julia to this role?* he will wonder. Could you be unhappy with David's past performance—is he no longer in your good graces? Even a securely attached employee might have some of these concerns—an anxiously attached employee certainly will.

So you should begin by trying to remove all the ambiguity you can. Meet with David before you announce Julia's new role, and explain your reasoning. Assure David that you are very pleased with his performance and that Julia's assignment should in no way be taken as evidence to the contrary. If possible, offer him an assignment that will reassure him by giving him greater responsibility or a chance to really shine.

With an avoidant perceiver, again, the word of the day is *patience*, because these people are super slow to warm up to others. It can take years. Here are a few other things to keep in mind:

- **Stress activates the avoidant lens.** Avoidant adults are particularly likely to distance themselves from other people during times of stress, so be aware that the avoidant perceiver might clam up during a particularly tough time.

- **Set expectations for yourself.** You aren't going to get a lot of warmth or support from an avoidant person, so it's important not to take that as necessarily a sign of hostility or dislike. (Remember, you've got a trust lens, too—and it is easy to get a distorted view of avoidant people when you're looking through it.)

- **Keep your own warmth in moderation.** Avoidant people are suspicious of too much ingratiation, and they don't respect it. You want to maintain a consistent room temperature in your dealings with them. Over time, your relationship will become warmer—just let it go at its own pace, and don't try to force intimacy or closeness.

Consider how you might treat a new avoidant-attached colleague, Margaret. She'll be working with you and the other members of your team on several projects. Your boss has just assigned her to take the lead on the next conference, and you think she might be feeling a little overwhelmed. Unfortunately, she's been distant and seems reluctant to ask for help. Now that you know about the avoidant lens, what should you do?

Margaret is almost certainly feeling stressed, which will just amplify her natural tendency to isolate herself. It will also increase her reluctance to ask for help, since she will then feel obligated to you—a relative stranger who she has no reason to assume she can trust.

It's fairly safe to assume that she needs your help—and to assume that she won't look either happy or grateful when you offer it. (Remember, it's not about you. Don't take it personally.) Try to refrain from being overly solicitous about it when you do offer help, because you don't want to come on too strong. You aren't trying to be her new best friend—just a colleague who can be counted on to lend a hand. Treat the whole thing like it's not a big deal, but be firm. Use a phrase like "Let me give you a hand with this," rather than "Would you like a hand with this?" If you make it a question, she'll almost certainly say "no thanks," no matter how much she needs it.

. . .

One thing to keep in mind about all four of these personality lenses—prevention, promotion, anxious, and avoidant—is that while the lenses are relatively stable, people can and do switch lenses throughout their lives. Experiences of loss can make a promotion-minded person more likely to wear the prevention lens, and experiences of rejection can make a securely attached person anxious or even avoidant. And it works in reverse—positive, responsive relationships can both help an anxious or avoidant person see that people can be trusted and help the person put down the lenses that are warping his or her social and emotional life. Perhaps you can even be a part of that process for others, now that you understand why they wear the lens that they do.

Key Takeaways

- Beginning in childhood, we develop mental models of what relationships are like—and whether other people can be trusted to be there for us when we need them. For roughly half of adults (i.e., the *securely attached*), their model is adaptive, in that they are trusting and make and maintain relationships easily. For the other half, things aren't so easy.

- *Anxiously attached* adults are, as the name implies, very anxious about their relationships. They desperately want intimacy, while being constantly worried that their relationship partners will reject them. They come off as needy, clingy, and emotionally volatile.

- To communicate effectively with an anxiously attached perceiver, it's essential to avoid ambiguity—take care that you don't inadvertently send a rejection signal (or one that could be construed as rejecting). Be reliable, be patient, and don't take a person's overblown reactions personally. It's not about you.

- Adults with *avoidant attachment* don't trust other people to be there for them at all, so they studiously avoid intimacy and other connection so as to never be vulner-able to rejection. They appear cold, aloof, and unfriendly.

- To communicate with the avoidant-attached, remember that a lack of warmth on their part does not necessarily signal hostility—it's more about caution. Don't try to warm things up by being overly friendly, because you will just make them uncomfortable. Relationships with these people take time to build, and it's necessary to take the long view.

Part IV

Being Seen, and Seeing Others, More Accurately

Chapter 9

Correcting Bad Impressions and Overcoming Misunderstandings

Your boss doesn't think you're particularly competent. Or your coworker thinks you're a pretentious ass. You've made a bad Phase 1 impression—probably because you were not yet familiar with the biases and lenses of perception—and now you want to repair the damage you've done. Well, desperate times call for desperate measures. You need to somehow get your perceiver to enter Phase 2, the correction phase, so that his or her impression of you will be revised to reflect you more accurately.

Once in Phase 2, the perceiver will be more likely to take into account the circumstances surrounding your actions (e.g., *Maybe she isn't incompetent . . . perhaps she's just new to this kind of task*). He or she may consider other likely motives for your behavior (e.g., *Maybe he's not really pretentious . . . he could be simply trying to appear knowledgeable, and he doesn't realize how it's coming across*). In Phase 2, perceivers are willing to entertain the possibility that they might have been wrong about you (e.g., *I should give him a second chance—not everyone makes a good first impression*).

People can and do revise their opinions of others all the time, and although first impressions are important, it's usually never too late to fix a negative one. The key is to understand what's going on "beneath the hood"—what it takes for the mind of the perceiver to change the picture the first impression has already painted of you.

I'm going to say this right up front: getting your perceiver to enter Phase 2 is going to be hard, and it will require patience, effort, and careful planning. There are, broadly speaking, two ways to approach the challenge.

Bombard Them with Overwhelming Evidence

One way to push your perceivers into Phase 2 is to bombard your perceivers with overwhelming evidence that their impression of you is wrong. In other words, keep piling it on until the cognitive misers can no longer selectively tune it out. The evidence has to be *attention getting*, because only information that is really inconsistent with their existing impression of you will likely get noticed. In other words, if you have given someone the impression that you're aloof and unfriendly, being a little friendlier next time isn't going to do a damn thing for you— it's just not going to even register.

So be prepared to go to extremes. For instance, imagine that your employee Carl has a well-deserved reputation for being late to work. You have spoken to him about it several times, and he has not improved. His behavior has led you to have serious questions about his competence and his commitment. Realizing this, Carl decides to turn over a new leaf and become punctual, hoping this will change your impression of him. Every day for a week, he arrives at work on time. Do you think this would lead you to see Carl in a new way? Do you think it would even register?

What if, instead of simply arriving on time, Carl starting arriving an hour early for work every day for a week. That would certainly register, because it represents a big change—a departure from your impression of him that's too big to ignore. You would naturally wonder, "What's up with Carl?" and pay closer attention to his behavior in the coming weeks to see if the change lasts. Carl's behavior would have successfully nudged you into Phase 2.

In a sense, this is what many actors are doing when they deliberately take on roles that require them to dramatically alter their appearance for the worse. When a beauty like Charlize Theron becomes almost unrecognizably ugly for her role as a serial killer in *Monster*, or when a handsome charmer like Matthew McConaughey loses forty-five pounds to play an AIDS-stricken man in *Dallas Buyers Club*, audiences and critics feel compelled to consider these actors with fresh eyes. Suddenly, the performer that you—and the Academy Awards voters—had pegged as "just another pretty face" or "that romantic-comedy guy" seems far more worthy of being taken seriously. When the evidence you provide the perceiver with is too attention getting or too unexpected to be ignored, the perceiver has no other way to make sense of it but to enter Phase 2 and reconsider his or her assumptions about you.

If you want to change an impression, the evidence should also be *plentiful*. If your boss thinks you are incompetent, then performing well once or twice—even if it's a genius-level performance—may not be enough to do the trick. It's too easy to write off a single piece of evidence as a fluke—an "even a blind pig finds an acorn now and then" kind of thing.

On the other hand, repeated, impressive displays of your extreme competence, non-pretentiousness, or friendliness (and, ideally, few distractions to compete for the perceiver's attention during these displays) will create too much cognitive dissonance in your perceiver's mind for him or her to dismiss or ignore, forcing the person to engage in Phase 2 to try to reduce the unpleasantness and get things right.

Because it requires so much evidence, in practice, the bombardment approach is often effort-intensive and time-consuming. Case in point: I have a good friend, "Patrick," who makes deeply terrible first impressions. Just god-awful, the worst I have ever seen. When he gets nervous, as he often does when meeting new people, he has a very strange and totally maladaptive defense mechanism: an uncanny ability to find something you feel particularly touchy about, and then make an insulting remark about it. It's like a moth to a flame.

People don't just form a negative impression of Patrick when they meet him—they actively *hate* him. But the thing is, the real Patrick is one of the most kind, loving, and loyal people you will ever meet. Once he stops being nervous and you really get to know him, you realize that he is the very opposite of what his first impression would lead you to believe. I've noticed that this process takes about six months, give or take—which is why his only friends tend to be the people who were forced to spend that much time with him, like his classmates and coworkers. It takes many, many instances of witnessing Patrick's good qualities to erase the memory of your first moments with him—moments that in no way represent the person he truly is.

Make Them *Want* to Revise Their Opinion of You

If you don't have six months to spare, you are going to have to go with this second option. When you can make your perceiver want to revise his or her opinion of you, you can achieve your aims faster and with less effort. But this approach requires you to make use of some clever strategizing.

Each of the strategies I'm about to describe has been shown to significantly increase the odds that a perceiver will enter Phase 2 processing and will form a more accurate (and often, more positive) impression of you. You can use them alone or in combination to increase the odds even further.

Activate the Perceiver's Goal of Egalitarianism, or Fairness

In general, people like to think of themselves as fair and unbiased. And if you ask them if they have the goal of judging people fairly and treating them accordingly, they will almost certainly tell you that yes, they do. Psychologists call this having an *egalitarian* goal.

Research suggests that when the egalitarian goal is strong and active—meaning that the perceiver is genuinely committed to fairness and that the goal has been activated in his or her mind in the current situation—the perceiver will spontaneously and automatically inhibit biases and stereotypes to a large degree.[1] In other words, the biases won't even come to mind, so they can't inappropriately influence perception. It's almost like skipping Phase 1 and heading directly to Phase 2, where the impression you create will be more accurate and more in keeping with your intentions.

The problem, of course, is that even when perceivers do have a strong egalitarian goal, they often aren't deliberately focused on that goal when they are judging you. After all, you probably want to be egalitarian, but when is the last time you thought to yourself, "I really want to judge this person fairly and accurately, without use of bias or stereotypes" when you met him or her for the first time? It's just not something any of us naturally do. So despite our desire to be unbiased, our egalitarian goal doesn't become *active*. The Phase 1 biases have free rein to muck things up, and we end up failing rather epically in the fairness department.

But as my good friend, Lehigh University psychologist Gordon Moskowitz, discovered, there are ways to make people aware of their egalitarian ideals—to activate the goal for them in a given interaction, in case they don't do it for themselves.[2] First, you can use the power of *labeling*. In general, people will try to conform to the labels they are given, provided that the labels are positive and not totally inconsistent with their existing views. For example, when individuals who contributed to a charity were told that they were "a generous donor," they gave significantly more money two weeks later when asked for another donation. It's as if they thought to themselves, *Well, after all, I* am *a generous donor, and giving more is what generous donors do.*[3]

You can harness this power by complimenting your perceiver on his or her "fairness," "unbiased assessment," "keen perception," or "uncanny accuracy" when it comes to perceiving others. If you don't know the perceiver well and would have no basis to make such a judgment, you can try a different approach—suggest that in the perceiver's line of work or in his or her position in the company, the ability to accurately and fairly assess others "must be a key skill to possess." You wouldn't be lying, since this is always a key skill to possess, no matter what someone does for a living. But by reminding the person of its importance, you will be activating the egalitarian goal that will lead him or her into Phase 2.

Interestingly, Moskowitz has found that there is an even more effective way to produce egalitarian perception—to remind the perceivers of times in the past that they have failed to be fair and unbiased. In his studies, he asks participants to reflect on a time in the past when their judgment of another person was influenced by the stereotype of their group—for instance, a time when they wondered if a female leader would be up to the job, simply because she was a woman, or a time when they felt threatened in the presence of a black man who hadn't actually done anything remotely threatening.[4] If we're honest, it's not hard for most of us to think of a time when we judged someone else in a way that we aren't proud of.

What Moskowitz consistently finds is that reminders of past failures to be fair create a powerful desire to be fair in the present. He refers to this process as *compensatory cognition,* because it is quite literally a (largely unconscious) attempt by the perceiver's brain to compensate for errors it has made in the past—to bring things back to the way they are supposed to be. Compensatory cognition results in strong activation of the egalitarian goal and a near complete inhibition of stereotypes and biases.

Now, I imagine you are wondering, how the heck do I remind someone of times when his or her judgment lacked fairness without, you know, having the person get really angry and hate me for it? Good question. You don't want to put your perceiver on the defensive, because the ego lens will kick in, and then you'll be toast. You must tread lightly.

Instead of hitting someone with an accusation, try opening up about some of your own challenges with fairness. Tell your own story about a time when you misjudged someone, by letting a stereotype or some other kind of bias get in the way. I have a whole catalog (I'm embarrassed to say) of such stories that I employ on these occasions:

> **The grad student from rural Pennsylvania:** I assumed she would be hopelessly boring and naive, only to find that she had a sharp wit and enough cynicism to rival any born-and-bred New Yorker.

> **The disheveled man in dirty sweatpants and T-shirt:** I found him wandering the halls at Columbia, and I nearly called Security on him—only to see him again a month later, delivering a talk to the entire department on the new complex statistic he had just invented. (This man, a noted psychologist and statistician, would later become one of my mentors. And yes, he would always look like that—though sometimes he would change T-shirts.)

The female postdoc with a shaved head and tattoos:
I avoided the woman from sheer terror, only to find her (once we were forced together) to be one of the sweetest, silliest people I have ever known. (Her hobbies—I kid you not—are knitting and Argentine tango. So you just never know.)

Once you have made it OK to admit to this kind of failure by sharing your own example, you can invite the perceivers to respond in kind by gently asking if anything like that has ever happened to them. Even if they don't share a story, it will get them thinking . . . and it will get their own fairness goal activated. In so doing, you create a window for them to see you in a new, more accurate way.

Notice When They Feel Out of Control

Human beings have a deep and fundamental desire for prediction and control. In order to survive, we human beings have evolved a universal, hardwired need to feel that we understand how the world works, that we can more or less anticipate what's going to happen, and that we can make things happen in our favor. This primal longing to be, in essence, captain of our own ship has come to have new implications in the modern world.

Decades of research show that people who perceive themselves to have more autonomy in their lives—more choices and less uncertainty at work and at home—are happier, less stressed, and better able to cope with life's hiccups than those who see themselves as a pawn of forces largely outside their control. People who feel in control also reach more of the goals they set for themselves and are better able to make and sustain major lifestyle changes when they set their minds to them.

Experiencing a lack of control, on the other hand, reliably leads to feelings of helplessness, apathy, and depression. In fact, low perceived control is one of the hallmarks of clinical depression—and the arrow of causality seems to point both ways: loss of control creates depression, and feelings of depression reduce our sense of control.

Of course, lots of other things diminish our sense of control, too. Natural disasters, unexpected loss, stressors, uncertainty, lack of choices, coercion, being micromanaged—any of these can make us feel relatively powerless and at the mercy of forces outside ourselves. And for most of us, that is a profoundly negative feeling.

It won't surprise you to learn that one of the very first things that happens when people experience a loss of control is that they try to get it back. And if they can't get it back by attacking the problem directly (e.g., telling the micromanaging boss, "I quit"), they will restore their sense of control in more subtle, largely unconscious ways. For example, people who chronically experience a loss of control are more likely to knock on wood or engage in other magical or superstitious thinking, to try to exert some influence over the otherwise uncontrollable.[5]

A big part of control is being able to successfully predict what's going to happen—so increasing your ability to predict what others might do or say is yet another way to restore a sense of control. Consequently, people who feel out of control often become more vigilant, put in more effort, and are more detail-oriented when observing others.[6]

For instance, in one study, researchers gave female undergraduates a series of puzzles to solve.[7] To solve them correctly, the students needed to recognize patterns across the series of puzzles—something they could only do if given accurate feedback after each puzzle. Some of these unfortunate volunteers did not receive accurate feedback—instead they received a mix of true and false feedback after each puzzle. Then, when asked to identify the total pattern after the last puzzle, they made a guess and were given no feedback at all about whether they were right or wrong. Unpredictable patterns and a lack of feedback is a great way to undermine a person's sense of control, and that's exactly what these young women reported feeling.

Then, all of the women were told that they would be performing a second task with a partner, and they were given the opportunity to request information about that partner in advance. The researchers found that those women who had a diminished sense of control consistently asked for more personal, diagnostic information about their future partner. To restore their sense of control, they sought to understand more thoroughly and accurately the person they would be working with.

While your perceiver is likely to go the extra mile to really "get you" when he or she is feeling out of control, it's not exactly easy (or, strictly speaking, ethical) to deliberately put another person into that state. Your best bet is to instead simply take advantage of times when you notice your perceiver is already feeling a bit out of control—times when he or she is stressed, anxious, or a bit down, whatever the reason.

When that happens, you can offer up "getting to know you accurately" as a way to take back the reins. I'm not suggesting you actually say that—in fact, you don't need to. Your stressed-out perceiver will naturally attempt to get a better handle on everything around him or her, including you. It's an automatic coping mechanism—we are all just wired that way.

For example, if your office is going through a particular period of uncertainty—such as a change initiative or new leadership—it could be a good time to approach a colleague you'd like to have a better impression of you. Mention that you'd like to get better acquainted—perhaps over lunch—because it's so much easier to work together when colleagues really know one another. "Really knowing someone" is a great way to increase one's sense of control, so this should be particularly appealing. (If you are already acquainted with the colleague—say you've been working together for a year—then you can propose lunch as a way to find ways to work together more effectively. This is another way to increase control.)

Consider another example. Let's say your boss seems overwhelmed with the number of projects on her plate. You could offer to lend a hand and could use the opportunity to showcase the skill set you want her to recognize—for instance, your organizational skills, or your initiative taking, or your resilience under pressure. Stepping up to help when a supervisor or colleague is in crisis is a great way to highlight your strengths when the person is most likely to notice.

Make Their Outcomes Dependent on You

In many ways the easiest and most direct way to get other people to want to perceive you correctly—to make the effort of Phase 2 processing worthwhile—is to create a state of interdependence between you and other people. Psychologists call this *outcome dependency*, and it has two basic forms.

You Are Going to Need Me

This is the stronger form, where I literally can't get what I want without cooperation from you. This is why the powerless pay such close attention to the powerful. And this is why individuals who must rely on a colleague or teammate to deliver will take the trouble to understand that person's character, intentions, and habits more accurately. The strong form of outcome dependency makes cooperation a necessity. I need to be able to predict your behavior, anticipate your wants and needs, and respond accordingly.

The need for accurate perception that real interdependence creates probably plays a big role in romantic relationships as well. In a couple's early days, they can afford to see one another through rose-colored glasses, only focusing on one another's best qualities and ignoring the other, less attractive bits because their lives are still relatively independent. But once that changes—once commitments increase, bills are shared, and there are children to raise—we literally cannot afford to paint mental pictures of our partners that are anything less than true. Romance may not fade as a consequence of knowing each other too well, but rather, we *must* know each other only too well if we are going to make interdependence work.

So when someone has formed a faulty impression of you, whatever the reason, it's in your interest to find ways to increase your mutual interdependence. Offer to help the person on a current project, or ask your supervisor if the two of you can be assigned to work on something together. (Supervisors love anything that smacks of team building, so they will like this idea.) Give your perceivers the best possible reason to want to

see you accurately—because they need you if they are going
to succeed.

You Are Going to Have to Deal with Me

Human beings have evolved lots of ways of dealing with hardship
and stress—skills and strategies that enable us to remain relatively happy and optimistic even when things are going very, very
wrong. Psychologists Timothy Wilson and Dan Gilbert refer to
these mechanisms collectively as the *psychological immune system*,
and it exists to protect us from extended bouts of strong negative
emotion. People are often, for instance, able to extract meaningful life lessons from failures that enable them to feel stronger and
smarter for having experienced them. They count their blessings
and focus on the part of the glass that is half full, rather than
half empty. They decide that, really, they are better off without
the relationship (or job) they have lost, because it wasn't making
them happy anyway. And when they know that they are going
to have to endure something fairly difficult or painful for quite a
while—like rehabilitation from an injury or four years of medical school—the most successful people find ways of thinking
about their goals that make the mountain easier to climb.

So, when you know that you are going to be seeing and
interacting on a regular basis with someone you strongly
dislike—when it is absolutely unavoidable—the psychological
immune system kicks in to convince you that it won't be so
bad. *He isn't really that awful, right?* you say to yourself. *Now
that I think about it, there was that one time he was sort of OK.*

A good friend of mine, "Jake," once used this strategy to
great effect. He was engaged to marry the daughter of a very
successful New York advertising executive, and the executive

in question was not happy about it. Jake, a native Texan, was a twenty-two-year-old recent college graduate with no significant career prospects and not a dollar to his name. The executive's daughter was herself only twenty, and the two had been dating for only a few months. But they were deeply in love and absolutely certain (as young people so often are) that they had each found The One.

So Jake decided that without warning, he would pack a bag and book a flight to New York. He arrived at his future father-in-law's doorstep and made it clear that he had no intention of leaving for at least a week—however long it took for them to get to know one another and for Jake to change the older man's mind. Jake felt certain that by sticking to the man like glue, Jake might eventually wear down the older man. And that's exactly what happened—anger turned to resignation and eventually even to liking. By the end of his ten-day visit, Jake had secured the executive's blessing. Once it was clear that resistance was futile, it seems the only sensible course of action was to give in and like the guy.

Strictly speaking, this strategy doesn't necessarily result in a more accurate view so much as a more positive view.[8] Once someone realizes that he or she is going to have to put up with you for a while, the person is more likely to want to see the best in you. So if you suspect that you have created a bad impression or that your perceiver just isn't noticing your good qualities, try to increase the amount of contact between the two of you. Stick to your perceiver like glue, and eventually the person will learn to like you, even if it kills him or her.

Here's a hypothetical: You have clearly rubbed your colleague Jason, the director of another division in your company, the wrong way. You can't put your finger on what exactly you did to earn his ire, but every time the two of you are in a meeting together, you can feel the coldness and distrust emanating from him, and it's directed at you. You have heard through the grapevine that Jason may take over for his boss when she retires next year, and that means he will be in a position to affect you and your work. You need to repair this relationship, before an increase in his relative power over you only makes it worse. The problem is that the two of you don't see much of one another and don't work together on any projects, so there is little opportunity for you to right this wrong.

The solution is to create more face time. You begin with a little investigating and find out that Jason works out in the company gym most mornings and eats in the company cafeteria at 1 p.m. on most days. So you move your schedule around accordingly. You make sure that he sees you each time you are in the gym or cafeteria, though you do *not* always approach him—after all, you do not want to come off like a stalker. Many times you simply smile and nod or do a quick wave. The idea is for him to register your presence, again and again. (You may have heard the expression "Familiarity breeds contempt," but what the research tells us is that in most cases, what familiarity breeds is *liking*. This happens partly because we are more comfortable with things that we've seen before and partly because we feel that if something or someone is going to be around a lot, we might as well like the person or thing. It's just easier that way.)

As you notice Jason beginning to thaw, it's OK to walk right up to him and engage him more often—asking if you can join him for lunch, for instance. The idea is not to be overly ingratiating or weirdly accommodating or to advertise your good qualities, but to just be your normal (hopefully friendly) self. He can find out on his own what there is to like about you, and now that you seem to be ever-present, he will be properly motivated to do so.

Remember, Phase 2 doesn't happen automatically. Your perceivers have to have the mental energy *and* the motivation to do the work. Bombarding them with attention-getting evidence of your true nature will do the trick, but that can take a lot of time—time you may not have to spare. In that case, reminding them of their desire to judge people fairly, encouraging them to restore their sense of control by knowing you accurately, and increasing your mutual interdependence will all serve to maximize their Phase 2 motivation. The only other thing you'll need, then, to correct their impression of you is a little patience. People rarely change their minds about something or someone overnight—but they do change, and now you have the tools to help that change along.

A Special Case: The Apology

You promised your boss you would complete an important assignment on time, and you realize you were wrong and it's going to be late. You leave a colleague out of the loop on a joint project, causing him to feel frustrated and a bit betrayed. It's time for a mea culpa.

Sometimes, the best way to get someone's attention—and really get the person to revise an opinion of you—is to own up to your behavior with an apology. But apologies are tricky things. Done right, they can resolve conflict, repair hurt feelings, foster forgiveness, and improve relationships. An apology can even keep you out of the courtroom. (Despite the fact that lawyers tend to caution their clients to avoid apologies like the plague, fearing that apologies are tantamount to an admission of guilt, studies show that when potential plaintiffs receive an apology, they are more likely to settle out of court for less money.)

But as anyone can tell you, apologies don't go so well. Ask Chip Wilson, the ousted Lululemon CEO discussed earlier in this book. Or John Edwards. Or Kanye West. (I could go on and on.) An apology is no guarantee that you'll find yourself out of hot water. Perhaps the person or persons you are seeking forgiveness from aren't really interested in forgiving, or perhaps the transgression itself is deemed simply unforgivable. But more often than not, your apology falls flat because you apologize the wrong way. Use these strategies to get the apology right:

- **Don't justify.** Most people make the mistake of making their apologies about themselves—about their own intentions, thoughts, and feelings.

    "I didn't mean to . . ."

    "I was trying to . . ."

    "I didn't realize . . ."

    "I had a good reason . . ."

    When you screw up, the victims of your screwup do not want to hear about you. So stop talking about yourself, and put the focus of your apology where it belongs: on them.

- **Imagine their perspective.** Specifically, focus on how they have been affected by your mistake, on how they are feeling, and on what they need from you in order to move forward. You need to take all ambiguity out of the situation, lest their lenses wreak havoc.

- **Acknowledge their feelings and values.** Your perceivers are experiencing a threat, so they need affirmation. By recognizing what they are feeling and encouraging them to talk about what is important to them, you will be taking important steps in healing the damage you've done.

- **Restore a sense of "us."** When you fail to deliver on your promises, or when you wrong another person in some way, it not only diminishes trust—it damages the sense of *us* that exists between you and your perceiver. You run the risk of becoming a *them*. Remind the injured party of your shared history, your commonalities, your shared goals. Reassure him or her that you are on the same team and have no intention of letting the team down again.

- **Know your audience.** It makes intuitive sense that the apology you give to your spouse for forgetting your anniversary should be different from the apology you give the stranger on the subway you spilled coffee on. But how should the apologies differ? Thanks to recent research on effective apologies, you can and should fine-tune your approach to apologizing, according to your relationship with the apology receiver.[9]

Compensation Versus Empathy in Apologies

The guy in the coffee-stained suit wants an *offer of compensation*. For strangers or mere acquaintances, offers of compensation are attempts to restore balance through some redeeming action. Sometimes the compensation is tangible, like paying to repair or replace your neighbor's fence when you inadvertently back your car into it, or running out to get your girlfriend a new phone when you accidentally drop hers into the toilet. Offers of compensation can also be more emotional or socially supportive—as in, "I'm sorry I acted like a jerk, and I'll make it up to you by being extra thoughtful from now on."

But if you are a partner, colleague, or friend, you need to offer an *expression of empathy*. The colleague you left out of the loop or the spouse whose feelings you hurt doesn't want compensation. Expressions of empathy involve taking the other person's perspective and recognizing and expressing concern over the suffering you caused. (For example, "I'm so sorry that I didn't appreciate all the effort you went to. You must have felt awful, and that's the last thing I want.") Through expressions of empathy, the victim feels understood and valued as a partner in the relationship, and trust is restored.

What if you've let the whole team down? Since in the workplace, we often operate as teams, if you've messed up, then chances are the entire group is affected. In team settings, people don't want compensation or empathy—they want an *acknowledgement of violated rules and norms*. You basically need to admit that you broke the code of behavior of your social group, your organization, or your society. (For example,

"I have a responsibility to my team/organization/family/community—and I should have known better." "I didn't just let myself down, I let others who count on me down.")

When you think about it, it's surprising that we're often so bad at apologizing. After all, we are frequently on the receiving end of apologies ourselves—so we should know what works and what doesn't, right? In reality, we often forget what it's like to be on the other side—whether we're trying to apologize, persuade, help, or motivate.

So when crafting your apology, remember to ask yourself, *Who am I talking to, and what are they looking for in my apology?* The guy on the subway doesn't want to hear that you "feel his pain"—but when you forget your spouse's birthday, your loved one definitely would like you to feel his or hers.

Conclusion

Becoming a Better Judge of Others—and of Yourself

You are almost at the end of this book, and up until now, I've focused more or less exclusively on how you can get other people to see you more positively or accurately—how you can come across to others the way you intend to. Successful communication just isn't possible without a clear picture of how other people perceive you. But there are two other elements of successful communication that I haven't addressed directly: accurately perceiving others and accurately perceiving yourself.

Seeing Others Accurately

Let's face it—it's not particularly fair to complain about other people not really "getting you" when you aren't really getting them either, is it? And beyond that, there are obvious advantages to reading other people—their intentions, their feelings, and their character—as accurately as possible. But you and I, as perceivers, are just as vulnerable to being influenced by faulty assumptions, biases, and lenses as everyone else is. We've got the same mental hardware as everyone else, we have the same limited time and energy, and so we take the same shortcuts without realizing it.

Only now, hopefully, you do realize it. And that's half the battle. Awareness of bias makes it easier to mitigate or root out bias entirely. What's the other half? Whenever you are forming an impression or making a judgment about a person, remember to use these strategies:

- **Take your time.** Don't rush to judgment. Keep in mind that your first impression of someone may be dead wrong, because there are always other possible interpretations of his or her behavior. Think about the circumstances and how they might have influenced the person's actions (e.g., "Maybe Susan isn't trying to be rude. Maybe she's just nervous meeting new people, and her fear and awkwardness is making her come off poorly. She might be quite different once you get to know her.").

- **Commit to being fair.** Remember that we all (or, at least most of us) want to be fair, but that doesn't mean we are actively pursuing that goal whenever we perceive another person. A simple reminder to yourself to be fair when you judge someone else is enough to activate the goal and diminish your unconscious bias. Make it a mantra, something you say before you walk into any meeting. Stick it to your computer with a Post-It note. The more you consciously think about being fair, the more accurate your perception will be.

- **Beware of confirmation bias.** Once we form an impression of someone, we tend to look selectively at his or her

behavior to find confirming evidence that our impression
is correct, rather than looking at all the evidence available.

Imagine that you are considering two candidates for a management position—Eliot and Joanna. You know them both,
but not particularly well. You are worried that Joanna may
not be assertive enough to be an effective manager—there was
that one time that she seemed reluctant to take the lead on a
project—so you are thinking of giving the promotion to Eliot.
(The stereotype that women are less assertive may well be bias-
ing your perception here.)

To evaluate this decision correctly, you need to consider four
kinds of evidence. When assertiveness was called for . . .

Instances where Joanna was *not* assertive	Instances where Joanna was assertive
Instances where Eliot was *not* assertive	Instances where Eliot was assertive

Thanks to confirmation bias, we tend to look only at
hypothesis-confirming evidence (i.e., instances where Joanna
was not assertive—just one of the four boxes above) and ignore
the rest.

So when you are making judgments about other people,
make sure you are checking all four quadrants—considering
evidence for and against your hypothesis and considering what
other people have done under similar circumstances.

Seeing Yourself Clearly

I wrote this book to help people understand why they are so
often misunderstood, because it happens a lot. But the truth is,

not every misunderstanding is . . . well, a misunderstanding. Sometimes, the perceiver is seeing the truth about you, and you are the one with blinders on.

Really knowing yourself is harder than you might think. As I've mentioned many times throughout this book, we don't always have access to what's going on in our own minds. And we are complicated creatures, with multiple selves to contend with. (Are you really the same person with your close friends that you are at work or with family?) We also have particular motivations—we want to see ourselves in certain ways. There's no objectivity in perception, whether you talking about perceiving others or perceiving yourself.

So how do you know if you are being misunderstood and misjudged or if you are fooling yourself? It's not easy to know, to be honest. And it's a topic that really deserves its own book. But one piece of advice I can give you is to look for consistency across perceivers. In other words, if everybody—your friends, your family, your colleagues—is making the same "mistake" about you, then it's probably not a mistake at all. And then it's time to go into Phase 2 for *you*, to question the assumptions you've been making about yourself and reconcile others' version of you with your own.

. . .

Perceiving people—including yourself—accurately is perhaps the most difficult thing we humans do. People are complicated, and their words and deeds are riddled with ambiguity and open to interpretation. We don't realize that's the case, because the way our brains are wired makes perception feel so obvious and effortless. But it's neither—which is why we so often screw it up.

If you want to come across the way you intend to—to have other people see you as you (think you) are or as you'd like to be seen—you are going to have to give them a hand. Remember that it doesn't help to blame the perceiver for getting you wrong. Instead, try making it easier for him or her to get you right.

Notes

Chapter 1

1. P. Baker and T. Gabriel, "With Biden Up Next to Debate, Obama's Aides Plot Comeback," *New York Times*, October 7, 2012, www.nytimes.com/2012/10/08/us/politics/biden-up-next-obamas-aides-plot-comeback.html?pagewanted=all; and A. Nagourney, A. Parker, J. Rutenberg, and J. Zeleny, "How a Race in the Balance Went to Obama," *New York Times*, November 7, 2012, www.nytimes.com/2012/11/08/us/politics/obama-campaign-clawed-back-after-a-dismal-debate.html?pagewanted=all&_r=0.

2. J. Alter, "Obama's Choke Revisited: What His First Debate Tells Us About His Troubled Second Term," *New Republic*, May 29, 2013, www.newrepublic.com/article/113287/obamas-denver-debate-choke-inside-debate-prep.

3. J. D. Vorauer and S. Claude, "Perceived Versus Actual Transparency of Goals in Negotiation," *Personality and Social Psychology Bulletin* 24, no. 4 (1998): 371–385.

4. D. C. Funder, ed., *Personality Judgment: A Realistic Approach to Person Perception* (Waltham, MA: Academic Press, 1999).

5. L. J. Human and J. C. Biesanz, "Targeting the Good Target: An Integrative Review of the Characteristics and Consequences of Being Accurately Perceived," *Personality and Social Psychology Review* 17, no. 3 (2013): 248–272.

6. D. Leising, O. Ostrovski, and J. Zimmermann, "'Are We Talking About the Same Person Here?' Interrater Agreement in Judgments of Personality Varies Dramatically with How Much the Perceivers Like the Targets," *Social Psychological and Personality Science* 40 (2012).

7. F. J. Bernieri, M. Zuckerman, R. Koestner, and R. Rosenthal, "Measuring Person Perception Accuracy: Another Look at Self-Other Agreement," *Personality and Social Psychology Bulletin* 20, no. 4 (1994): 367–378.

8. F. D. Fincham, S. R. Beach, and D. H. Baucom, "Attribution Processes in Distressed and Nondistressed Couples: IV. Self–Partner Attribution Differences," *Journal of Personality and Social Psychology* 52, no. 4 (1987): 739.

Chapter 2

1. See http://www.natgeotv.com/ca/human-shark-bait/facts.
2. E. Jones et al., "Pattern of Performance and Ability Attribution: An Unexpected Primacy Effect," *Journal of Personality and Social Psychology* 10, no. 4. (1968): 317–340.
3. A. Zebrowitz and S. M. McDonald, "The Impact of Litigants' Baby-Facedness and Attractiveness on Adjudications in Small Claims Courts," *Law and Human Behavior* 15, no. 6 (1991): 603–623.
4. R. J. Sternberg, "A Systems Model of Leadership: WICS," *American Psychologist* 62, no. 1 (2007): 34.
5. J. S. Mueller, J. A. Goncalo, and D. Kamdar, "Recognizing Creative Leadership: Can Creative Idea Expression Negatively Relate to Perceptions of Leadership Potential?" *Journal of Experimental Social Psychology* 47, no. 2 (2011): 494–498.
6. A. R. Pratkanis, "The Attitude Heuristic and Selective Fact Identification," *British Journal of Social Psychology* 27, no. 3 (1988): 257–263.
7. L. Ross, "The False Consensus Effect: An Egocentric Bias in Social Perception and Attribution Processes," *Journal of Experimental Social Psychology* 13, no. 3 (1977): 279–301.
8. C. Heath, "On the Social Psychology of Agency Relationships: Lay Theories of Motivation Overemphasize Extrinsic Incentives," *Organizational Behavior and Human Decision Processes* 78, no. 1 (1999): 25–62.
9. R. Rosenblatt, "The 11th Commandment," *Family Circle*, December 21, 1993: 30–32.

Chapter 3

1. K. Montee, "Astaire: He Danced His Way into Our Hearts," *Fort Lauderdale (FL) Sun-Sentinel*, June 23, 1987, http://articles.sun-sentinel.com/1987-06-23/features/8702230907_1_fred-astaire-top-hat-dancing.
2. D. T. Gilbert, "Ordinary Personology," *The Handbook of Social Psychology* 2 (1998): 89–150.
3. D. T. Gilbert, B. W. Pelham, and D. S. Krull, "On Cognitive Busyness: When Person Perceivers Meet Persons Perceived," *Journal of Personality and Social Psychology* 54, no. 5 (1988): 733.
4. D. Kahneman, *Thinking, Fast and Slow* (New York: Farrar, Straus, and Girous, 2011).
5. D. T. Gilbert, "Ordinary Personology," in *Handbook of Social Psychology*, vol. 2, eds. S. T. Fiske, D. T. Gilbert, and G. Lindzey (New York: McGraw-Hill, 1998), 97.

6. E. E. Jones and V. A. Harris, "The Attribution of Attitudes," *Journal of Experimental Social Psychology* 3, no. 1 (1967): 1–24.

7. M. Bertrand and S. Mullainathan, "Are Emily and Greg More Employable Than Lakisha and Jamal? A Field Experiment on Labor Market Discrimination" (working paper no. 9873, National Bureau of Economic Research, 2003).

8. J. Creswell and L. Thomas Jr., "The Talented Mr. Madoff," *New York Times*, January 24, 2009, www.nytimes.com/2009/01/25/business/25bernie.html?pagewanted=all.

9. G. V. Bodenhausen, "Stereotypes as Judgmental Heuristics: Evidence of Circadian Variations in Discrimination," *Psychological Science* 1, no. 5 (1990): 319–322.

10. P. G. Devine, "Stereotypes and Prejudice: Their Automatic and Controlled Components," *Journal of Personality and Social Psychology* 56, no. 1 (1989): 5.

Chapter 4

1. CNN, "Transcript: Bush, Putin News Conference," CNN.com, June 18, 2001, http://edition.cnn.com/2001/WORLD/europe/06/18/bush.putin.transcript/.

2. G. Casimir, K. Lee, and M. Loon, "Affective Commitment and Knowledge Sharing: Influence of Trust and the Perceived Cost of Knowledge Sharing," *Journal of Knowledge Management* 16, no. 5 (2012): 740–753.

3. R. D. Costigan et al., "Revisiting the Relationship of Supervisor Trust and CEO Trust to Turnover Intentions," *Journal of World Business* 46, no. 1 (2011): 74–83.

4. J. Guinot, R. Chiva, and V. Roca-Puig, "Interpersonal Trust, Stress, and Satisfaction at Work: An Empirical Study," *Personnel Review* 43 (2014).

5. C. Crossley, C. Cooper, and T. Wernsing, "Making Things Happen through Challenging Goals: Leader Proactivity, Trust, and Business Unit Performance," *Journal of Applied Psychology* 98, no. 3 (2013): 540–549.

6. S. T. Fiske, A. J. Cuddy, and P. Glick, "Universal Dimensions of Social Cognition: Warmth and Competence," *Trends in Cognitive Sciences* 11, no. 2 (2007): 77–83.

7. A. J. Cuddy, M. Kohut, and J. Neffinger, "Connect, Then Lead," *Harvard Business Review* 91, no. 7 (2013): 54–61.

8. D. S. Holoien and S. T. Fiske, "Downplaying Positive Impressions: Compensation Between Warmth and Competence in Impression Management," *Journal of Experimental Social Psychology* 49 (2013): 33–41.

9. R. Gifford, "A Lens-Mapping Framework for Understanding the Encoding and Decoding of Interpersonal Dispositions in Nonverbal Behavior," *Journal of Personality and Social Psychology* 66, no. 2 (1994): 398–412.

10. A. W. Brooks, H. Dai, and M. E. Schweitzer, "I'm Sorry About the Rain! Superfluous Apologies Demonstrate Empathic Concern and Increase Trust," *Social Psychological and Personality Science* 5, no. 4 (2013): 467–474.

11. B. C. Gunia, J. M. Brett, and A. Nandkeolyar, "Trust Me, I'm a Negotiator: Using Cultural Universals to Negotiate Effectively, Globally," *Organizational Dynamics* 43 (2014): 27–36.

12. N. A. Murphy, "Appearing Smart: The Impression Management of Intelligence, Person Perception Accuracy, and Behavior in Social Interaction," *Personality and Social Psychology Bulletin* 33, no. 3 (2007): 325–339.

13. F. Righetti and C. Finkenauer, "If You Are Able to Control Yourself, I Will Trust You: The Role of Perceived Self-control in Interpersonal Trust," *Journal of Personality and Social Psychology* 100, no. 5 (2011): 874.

14. Ibid.

15. T. Chamorro-Premuzic and A. Furnham, *Personality and Intellectual Competence* (East Sussex, UK: Psychology Press, 2014).

16. A. J. Cuddy, C. A. Wilmuth, and D. R. Carney, "The Benefit of Power Posing Before a High-Stakes Social Evaluation" (working paper, Harvard Business School, Boston, 2012).

17. Z. L. Tormala, J. S. Jayson, and M. I. Norton, "The Preference for Potential," *Journal of Personality and Social Psychology* 103, no. 4 (2012): 567.

18. Holoien and Fiske, "Downplaying Positive Impressions."

19. A. J. Cuddy, Susan T. Fiske, and P. Glick, "Warmth and Competence as Universal Dimensions of Social Perception: The Stereotype Content Model and the BIAS Map," in *Advances in Experimental Social Psychology*, vol. 40, ed. M. P. Zanna (New York: Academic Press, 2008), 61–149.

20. C. M. Judd, L. James-Hawkins, V. Yzerbyt, and Y. Kashima, "Fundamental Dimensions of Social Judgment: Understanding the Relations Between Judgments of Competence and Warmth," *Journal of Personality and Social Psychology* 89 (2005): 899–913.

Chapter 5

1. D. Adams, *Dirk Gently's Holistic Detective Agency* (New York: Simon & Schuster, 1987).

2. J. C. Magee and P. K. Smith, "The Social Distance Theory of Power," *Personality and Social Psychology Review* 17, no. 2 (2013): 158–186.

3. C. Anderson and A. D. Galinsky, "Power, Optimism, and Risk Taking," *European Journal of Social Psychology* 36, no. 4 (2006): 511–536.

4. P. K. Piff et al., "Higher Social Class Predicts Increased Unethical Behavior," *Proceedings of the National Academy of Sciences* 109, no. 11 (2012): 4086–4091.

5. J. Hogeveen, M. Inzlicht, and S. S. Obhi, "Power Changes How the Brain Responds to Others," *Journal of Experimental Psychology: General* 143, no. 2 (2014): 755–762.

6. S. A. Goodwin et al., "Power Can Bias Impression Processes: Stereotyping Subordinates by Default and by Design," *Group Processes and Intergroup Relations* 3, no. 3 (2000): 227–256.

7. Ibid.

8. R. Rodríguez-Bailón, M. Moya, and V. Yzerbyt, "Cuando el poder ostentado es inmerecido: sus efectos sobre la percepción y los juicios sociales" [When power is undeserved: its effects on perception and social judgments], *Psicothema* 18, no. 2 (2006): 194–199.

9. J. R. Overbeck and B. Park, "Powerful Perceivers, Powerless Objects: Flexibility of Powerholders' Social Attention," *Organizational Behavior and Human Decision Processes* 99, no. 2 (2006): 227–243.

Chapter 6

1. M. Agthe, M. Spörrle, and J. K. Maner, "Does Being Attractive Always Help? Positive and Negative Effects of Attractiveness on Social Decision Making," *Personality and Social Psychology Bulletin* 37, no. 8 (2011): 1042–1054.

2. Ibid.

3. N. D. Weinstein, "Unrealistic Optimism About Susceptibility to Health Problems," *Journal of Behavioral Medicine* 5, no. 4 (1982): 441–460.

4. In D. G. Myers, *Social Psychology*, 9th ed. (New York: McGraw Hill, 2007).

5. A. Tesser, M. Millar, and J. Moore, "Some Affective Consequences of Social Comparison and Reflection Processes: The Pain and Pleasure

of Being Close," *Journal of Personality and Social Psychology* 54, no. 1 (1988): 49.

6. M. Hewstone, M. Rubin, and H. Willis, "Intergroup Bias," *Annual Review of Psychology* 53, no. 1 (2002): 575–604.

7. S. Fein and S. J. Spencer, "Prejudice as Self-Image Maintenance: Affirming the Self through Derogating Others" *Journal of Personality and Social Psychology* 73, no. 1 (1997): 31.

8. R. B. Cialdini and K. D. Richardson, "Two Indirect Tactics of Image Management: Basking and Blasting," *Journal of Personality and Social Psychology* 39, no. 3 (1980): 406.

9. Ari Emanuel, quoted in E. Bumiller, "The Brothers Emanuel," *New York Times*, June 15, 1997, www.nytimes.com/1997/06/15/magazine/the-brothers-emanuel.html?src=pm&pagewanted=2.

10. H. Tajfel and J. C. Turner, "The Social Identity Theory of Intergroup Behavior," in *Political Psychology: Key Readings*, eds. J. T. Jost and J. Sidanius (New York: Psychology Press, 2004).

11. H. Tajfel, "Social Psychology of Intergroup Relations," *Annual Review of Psychology* 33, no. 1 (1982): 1–39.

Chapter 7

1. E. T. Higgins, "Promotion and Prevention: Regulatory Focus as a Motivational Principle," *Advances in Experimental Social Psychology* 30 (1998): 1–46.

2. H. G. Halvorson and E. T. Higgins, *Focus: Use Different Ways of Seeing the World for Success and Influence* (New York: Penguin, 2013).

3. P. B. Baltes, U. M. Staudinger, and U. Lindenberger, "Lifespan Psychology: Theory and Application to Intellectual Functioning," *Annual Review of Psychology* 50, no. 1 (1999): 471–507.

4. E. T. Higgins, J. Shah, and R. Friedman, "Emotional Responses to Goal Attainment: Strength of Regulatory Focus as Moderator," *Journal of Personality and Social Psychology* 72, no. 3 (1997): 515.

5. D. Van Dijk and A. N. Kluger, "Feedback Sign Effect on Motivation: Is It Moderated by Regulatory Focus?" *Applied Psychology* 53, no. 1 (2004): 113–135.

6. H. Plessner et al., "Regulatory Fit as a Determinant of Sport Performance: How to Succeed in a Soccer Penalty-Shooting," *Psychology of Sport and Exercise* 10, no. 1 (2009): 108–115.

7. Ibid.

8. V. K. Bohns et al., "Opposites Fit: Regulatory Focus Complementarity and Relationship Well-Being," *Social Cognition* 31, no. 1 (2013): 1–14.

9. J. Cesario, H. Grant, and E. T. Higgins, "Regulatory Fit and Persuasion: Transfer from 'Feeling Right,'" *Journal of Personality and Social Psychology* 86, no. 3 (2004): 388.

Chapter 8

1. J. Bowlby, *A Secure Base: Parent-Child Attachment and Healthy Human Development* (New York: Basic Books, 1988).

2. C. Hazan and P. Shaver, "Romantic Love Conceptualized as an Attachment Process," *Journal of Personality and Social Psychology* 52, no. 3 (1987): 511.

3. K. Bartholomew and P. R. Shaver, "Methods of Assessing Adult Attachment," in *Attachment Theory and Close Relationships*, ed. J. A. Simpson and W. S. Rholes (New York: Guilford, 1998), 25–45.

4. Hazan and Shaver, "Romantic Love Conceptualized as an Attachment Process."

5. Bartholomew and Shaver, "Methods of Assessing Adult Attachment."

6. S. R. Levy, O. Ayduk, and G. Downey, "The Role of Rejection Sensitivity in People's Relationships with Significant Others and Valued Social Groups," in *Interpersonal Rejection*, ed. M. R. Leary (New York: Oxford University Press, 2001), 251.

7. G. Downey and S. I. Feldman, "Implications of Rejection Sensitivity for Intimate Relationships," *Journal of Personality and Social Psychology* 70, no. 6 (1996): 1327.

8. Bartholomew and Shaver, "Methods of Assessing Adult Attachment."

Chapter 9

1. G. B. Moskowitz and P. Li, "Egalitarian Goals Trigger Stereotype Inhibition: A Proactive Form of Stereotype Control," *Journal of Experimental Social Psychology* 47, no. 1 (2011): 103–116.

2. G. B. Moskowitz, P. Li, C. Ignarri, and J. Stone, "Compensatory Cognition Associated with Egalitarian Goals," *Journal of Experimental Social Psychology* 47, no. 2 (2011): 365–370.

3. J. M. Burger and D. F. Caldwell, "The Effects of Monetary Incentives and Labeling on the Foot-in-the-Door Effect: Evidence for a Self-Perception Process," *Basic and Applied Social Psychology* 25, no. 3 (2003): 235–241.

4. Moskowitz, Li, Ignarri, and Stone, "Compensatory Cognition."

5. G. Keinan, "The Effects of Stress and Desire for Control on Superstitious Behavior," *Personality and Social Psychology Bulletin* 28, no. 1 (2002): 102–108.

6. L. Hildebrand-Saints and G. Weary, "Depression and Social Information Gathering," *Personality and Social Psychology Bulletin* 15, no. 2 (1989): 150–160.

7. W. B. Swann, B. Stephenson, and T. S. Pittman, "Curiosity and Control: On the Determinants of the Search for Social Knowledge," *Journal of Personality and Social Psychology* 40, no. 4 (1981): 635.

8. S. C. Thompson and M. M. Schlehofer, "The Many Sides of Control Motivation," in *Handbook of Motivation Science*, eds. James Y. Shah and Wendi L. Gardner (New York: Guilford Press, 2008), 41.

9. R. Fehr, M. J. Gelfand, and M. Nag, "The Road to Forgiveness: A Meta-analytic Synthesis of Its Situational and Dispositional Correlates," *Psychological Bulletin* 136, no. 5 (2010): 894.

Index

Acknowledgments

This was a tremendously fun book to write, in no small part because of the terribly clever people who helped me do it. At Harvard Business Review Press, I am grateful for the keen eye, sharp wit, and endless enthusiasm of my editor and wordsmith Sarah Green, as well as the guiding wisdom of Tim "The Enchanter" Sullivan, who shepherded me through the process from beginning to end, and warned me about the rabbits. I am also grateful to production editor Jen Waring, publicist Nina Nocciolino, and many others at HBRP who worked so hard on this project.

Thank you to the amazing Dorie Clark and an anonymous reviewer for the insightful comments and suggestions on an early draft. And thank you for hating the original title. You were so very right. I see that now.

As ever, I am grateful to my extraordinary agent and dear friend Giles Anderson. The time and effort he has put into supporting me and my work—including this book—is astounding. I don't know how he does it all. I think he may have cloned himself.

This book would not have been possible without the hundreds of social and cognitive psychologists upon whose research it was based. We human beings are very tricky creatures to study, and there is so much about ourselves we still don't know. Thank you for continuing to shine your light into that darkness.

And finally, I thank my family—especially my mother, who is my most steadfast cheerleader and most critical reader, and my husband, who came up with the idea for this book.

You really do have to read this one, Jonathan.

About the Author

HEIDI GRANT HALVORSON, PhD, is Associate Director of Columbia Business School's Motivation Science Center and author of the international bestsellers *Nine Things Successful People Do Differently, Succeed: How We Can Reach Our Goals,* and *Focus: Use Different Ways of Seeing the World for Success and Influence* (with E. Tory Higgens).

She is a frequent contributor to *Harvard Business Review, Fast Company, 99U, The Atlantic,* and *Psychology Today.*

Heidi is also Senior Consultant at the NeuroLeadership Institute, where she works with organizations to develop strategies to break unconscious bias in decision making and to foster an organizational growth mind-set. She earned her PhD from Columbia University, working with Carol Dweck (author of *Mindset: The New Psychology of Success*).

Heidi and her family live in Pelham, NY.

Visit her website: heidigranthalvorson.com.